THE MILLIONAIRE BABY

By

ANNA KATHARINE GREEN

Double9
BOOKS

The Millionaire Baby

by **Anna Katharine Green**

ISBN: 978-93-58711-97-4

Published by

DOUBLE 9 BOOKS

2/13-B, Ansari Road, Daryaganj
New Delhi – 110002
info@double9books.com
www.double9books.com
Tel. 011-40042856

ABOUT THE AUTHOR

The American author Anna Katharine Green (1846–1955), who is recognized as one of the forerunners of detective fiction, was raised in a sophisticated and educated household and was born in Brooklyn, New York. Her debut book, "The Leavenworth Case," which was released in 1878, quickly rose to popularity. She produced countless short pieces in the genre in addition to almost 40 books. Intricate riddles, brilliant storytelling, and the use of forensic evidence were hallmarks of her books, which also often included characters like detective Ebenezer Gryce and the single sleuth Amelia Butterworth. Along with her contributions to the genre, Green pioneered the exploration of gender and social class issues in mysteries, often utilizing her characters to remark on societal injustices. She was on the executive committee of the New York State Suffrage Association and sponsored issues including public health and education, demonstrating her commitment to women's suffrage and charity. Her contributions to the detective fiction genre are still respected and recognized in modern times.

CONTENTS

I-TWO LITTLE SHOES

The morning of August eighteenth, 190-, was a memorable one to me. For two months I had had a run of bad luck. During that time I had failed to score in at least three affairs of unusual importance, and the result was a decided loss in repute as well as great financial embarrassment. As I had a mother and two sisters to support and knew but one way to do it, I was in a state of profound discouragement. This was before I took up the morning papers. After I had opened and read them, not a man in New York could boast of higher hopes or greater confidence in his power to rise by one bold stroke from threatened bankruptcy to immediate independence.

The paragraph which had occasioned this amazing change must have passed under the eyes of many of you. It created a wide-spread excitement at the time and raised in more than one breast the hope of speedy fortune. It was attached to, or rather introduced, the most startling feature of the week, and it ran thus:

A FORTUNE FOR A CHILD.

By cable from Southampton.

A reward of five thousand dollars is offered, by Philo Ocumpaugh, to whoever will give such information as will lead to the recovery, alive or dead, of his six-year-old daughter, Gwendolen, missing since the afternoon of August the 16th, from her home in – –on-the-Hudson, New York, U. S. A.

Fifty thousand dollars additional and no questions asked if she is restored unharmed within the week to her mother at Homewood.

All communications to be addressed to Samuel Atwater, – –on-the-Hudson.

A minute description of the child followed, but this did not interest me, and I did not linger over it. The child was no stranger to me. I knew her well and consequently was quite aware of her personal characteristics. It was the great amount offered for her discovery and restoration which moved me so deeply. Fifty thousand dollars! A fortune for any man. More than a fortune to me, who stood in such need of ready money. I was determined to win this extraordinary sum. I had my reason for hope and, in the light of this unexpectedly munificent reward, decided to waive all the considerations which had hitherto prevented me from stirring in the matter.

There were other reasons less selfish which gave impetus to my resolve. I had done business for the Ocumpaughs before and been well treated in the transaction. I recognized and understood both Mr. Ocumpaugh's peculiarities and those of his admired and devoted wife. As man and woman they were kindly, honorable and devoted to many more interests than those connected with their own wealth. I also knew their hearts to be wrapped up in this child, — the sole offspring of a long and happy union, and the actual as well as prospective inheritor of more millions than I shall ever see thousands, unless I am fortunate enough to solve the mystery now exercising the sympathies of the whole New York public.

You have all heard of this child under another name. From her birth she has been known as the Millionaire Baby, being the direct heir to three fortunes, two of which she had already received. I saw her first when she was three years old—a cherubic little being, lovely to look upon and possessing unusual qualities for so young a child. Indeed, her picturesque beauty and appealing ways would have attracted all eyes and won all hearts, even if she had not represented in her small person the wealth both of the Ocumpaugh and Rathbone families. There was an individuality about her, combined with sensibilities of no ordinary nature, which, fully accounted for the devoted affection with which she was universally regarded; and when she suddenly disappeared, it was easy to comprehend, if one did not share, the thrill of horror which swept from one end of our broad continent to the other. Those who knew the parents, and those who did not, suffered an equal pang at the awful thought of this petted innocent lost in the depths of the great unknown, with only the false caresses of her abductors to comfort her for the deprivation of all those delights which love and unlimited means could provide to make a child of her years supremely happy.

Her father — and this was what gave the keen edge of horror to the whole occurrence—was in Europe when she disappeared. He had been cabled at once and his answer was the proffered reward with which I have opened this history. An accompanying despatch to his distracted wife announced his relinquishment of the project which had taken him abroad and his immediate return on the next steamer sailing from Southampton. As this chanced to be the fastest on the line, we had reason to expect him in six days; meanwhile —

But to complete my personal recapitulations. When the first news of this startling abduction flashed upon my eyes from the bulletin boards, I looked on the matter as one of too great magnitude to be dealt with by any but the metropolitan police; but as time passed and further details of the strange and seemingly inexplicable affair came to light, I began to feel the stirring of the detective instinct within me (did I say that I was connected with a private detective agency of some note in the metropolis?) and a desire, quite apart from any mere humane interest in the event itself, to locate the intelligence back of such a desperate crime: an intelligence so keen that, up to the present moment, if we may trust the published accounts of the affair, not a clue had been unearthed by which its author could be traced, or the means employed for carrying off this petted object of a thousand cares.

To be sure, there was a theory which eliminated all crime from the occurrence as well as the intervention of any one in the child's fate: she might have strayed down to the river and been drowned. But the probabilities were so opposed to this supposition, that the police had refused to embraçe it, although the mother had accepted it from the first, and up to the present moment, or so it was stated, had refused to consider any other. As she had some basis for this conclusion—I am still quoting the papers, you understand—I was not disposed to ignore it in the study I proceeded to make of the situation. The details, as I ran them over in the hurried trip I now made up the river to − −, were as follows:

On the afternoon of Wednesday, August sixteenth, 190-, the guests assembled in Mrs. Ocumpaugh's white and gold music-room were suddenly thrown into confusion by the appearance among them of a young girl in a state of great perturbation, who, running up to the startled hostess, announced that Gwendolen, the petted darling of the house, was missing from the bungalow where she had been lying asleep, and could not be found, though a dozen men had been out on search.

The wretched mother, who, as it afterward transpired, had not only given the orders by which the child had been thus removed from the excitement up at the house, but had actually been herself but a few moments before to see that the little one was well cared for and happy, seemed struck as by a mortal blow at these words and, uttering a heart-rending scream, ran out on the lawn. A crowd of guests rushed after her, and as they followed her flying figure across the lawn to the small copse in which lay hidden this favored retreat, they could hear, borne back on the wind, the wild protests of the young nurse, that she had left the child for a minute only and then to go no farther than the bench running along the end of the bungalow facing the house; that she had been told she could sit there and listen to the music, but that she never would have left the child's side for a minute if she had not supposed she would hear her least stir—protests which the mother scarcely seemed to heed, and which were presently lost in the deep silence which fell on all, as, brought to a stand in the thick shrubbery surrounding the bungalow, they saw the mother stagger up to the door, look in and turn toward them with death in her face.

"The river!" she gasped, "the river!" and heedless of all attempt to stop her, heedless even of the efforts made by the little one's nurse to draw her attention to the nearness of a certain opening in the high hedge marking off the Ocumpaugh grounds on this side, she ran down the bank in the direction of the railway, but fainted before she had more than cleared the thicket. When they lifted her up, they all saw the reason for this. She had come upon a little shoe which she held with frantic clutch against her breast—her child's shoe, which, as she afterward acknowledged, she had loosened with her own hand on the little one's foot.

Of course, after this the whole hillside was searched down to the fence which separated it from the railroad track. But no further trace of the missing child was found, nor did it appear possible to any one that she could have strayed away in this direction. For not only was the bank exceedingly steep and the fence at its base impassable, but a gang of men, working as good fortune would have it, at such a point on the road below as to render it next to impossible for her to have crossed the track within a half-mile either way without being observed, had one and all declared that not one of them had seen her or any other person descend the slope.

This, however, made but little impression on the mother. She would listen to no hints of abduction, but persisted in her declaration that the river had swallowed her darling, and would neither rest nor turn her head from its waters till some half a dozen men about the place had been set systematically to work to drag the stream.

Meanwhile, the police had been notified and the whole town aroused. The search, which had been carried on up to this time in a frantic but desultory way, now became methodical. Nor was it confined to the Ocumpaugh estate. All the roads and byways within half a mile either way were covered by a most careful investigation. All the near-by houses were entered, especially those which the child was most in the habit of frequenting, but no one had seen her, nor could any trace of her presence be found. At five o'clock all hope of her return was abandoned and, much against Mrs. Ocumpaugh's wish, who declared that the news of the child's death would affect her father far less than the dreadful possibilities of an abduction, the exact facts of the case had been cabled to Mr. Ocumpaugh.

The night and another day passed, bringing but little relief to the situation. Not an eye had as yet been closed in Homewood, nor had the search ceased for an instant. Not an inch of the great estate had been overlooked, yet men could still be seen beating the bushes and peering into all the secluded spots which once had formed the charm of this delightful place. As on the land, so on the river. All the waters in the dock had been dragged, yet the work went on, some said under the very eye of Mrs. Ocumpaugh. But there was no result as yet.

In the city the interest was intense. The telegraph at police headquarters had been clicking incessantly for thirty-six hours under the direction, some said, of the superintendent himself. Everything which could be done had been done, but as yet the papers were able to report nothing beyond some vague stories of a child, with its face very much bound up, having been seen at the heels of a woman in the Grand Central Station in New York, and hints of a covered wagon, with a crying child inside, which had been driven through Westchester County at a great pace shortly before sunset on the previous day, closely followed by a buggy with the storm-apron up, though the sun shone and there was not a cloud in the sky; but nothing definite, nothing which could give hope to the distracted mother or do more than divide the attention of the police between two different but equally tenable theories. Then came the cablegram from Mr. Ocumpaugh, which threw amateur as well as professional detectives into the field. Among the latter was myself; which naturally brings me back once more to my own conclusions.

Of one thing I felt sure. Very early in my cogitations, before we had quitted the Park Avenue tunnel in fact, I had decided in my own mind that if I were to succeed in locating the lost heiress, it must be by subtler methods than lay open to the police. I was master of such methods (in this case at least), and though one of many owning to similar hopes on this very train which was rushing me through to Homewood, I had no feeling but that of confidence in a final success. How well founded this confidence was, will presently appear.

The number of seedy-looking men with a mysterious air who alighted in my company at — — station and immediately proceeded to make their way up the steep street toward Homewood, warned me that it would soon be extremely difficult for any one to obtain access to the parties most interested in the child's loss. Had I not possessed the advantage of being already known to Mrs. Ocumpaugh, I should have immediately given up all hope of ever obtaining access to her presence; and even with this fact to back me, I approached the house with very little confidence in my ability to win my way through the high iron gates I had so frequently passed before without difficulty.

And indeed I found them well guarded. As I came nearer, I could see man after man being turned away, and not till my card had been handed in, and a hurried note to boot, did I obtain permission to pass the first boundary. Another note secured me admission to the house, but there my progress stopped. Mrs. Ocumpaugh had already been interviewed by five reporters and a special agent from the New York police. She could see no one else at present. If, however, my business was of importance, an opportunity would be given me to see Miss Porter. Miss Porter was her companion and female factotum.

As I had calculated upon having a half-dozen words with the mother herself, I was greatly thrown out by this; but going upon the principle that "half a loaf was better than no bread," I was about to express a desire to see Miss Porter, when an incident occurred which effectually changed my mind in this regard.

The hall in which I was standing and which communicated with the side door by which I had entered, ended in a staircase, leading, as I had reason to believe, to the smaller and less pretentious rooms in the rear of the house. While I hesitated what reply to give the girl awaiting my decision, I caught the sound of soft weeping from the top of this staircase, and presently beheld the figure of a young woman coming slowly down, clad in coat and hat and giving every evidence both in dress and manner of leaving for good. It was Miss Graham, a young woman who held the position of nursery-governess to the child. I had seen her before, and had no small admiration for her, and the sensations I experienced at the sight of her leaving the house where her services were apparently no longer needed, proved to me, possibly for the first time, that I had more heart in my breast than I had ever before realized. But it was not this which led me to say to the maid standing before me that I preferred to see Mrs. Ocumpaugh herself, and would call early the next day. It was the thought that this sorrowing girl would have to pass the gauntlet of many prying eyes on her way to the station and that she might be glad of an escort whom she knew and had shown some trust in. Also, — but the reasons behind thatalsowill soon become sufficiently apparent.

I was right in supposing that my presence on the porch outside would be a pleasing surprise to her. Though her tears continued to flow she accepted my proffered companionship with gratitude, and soon we were passing side by side across the lawn toward a short cut leading down the bank to the small flag-station used by the family and by certain favored neighbors. As we threaded the shrubbery, which is very thick about the place, she explained to me the cause of her abrupt departure. The sight of her, it seems, had become insupportable to Mrs. Ocumpaugh. Though no blame could be rightfully attached to her, it was certainly true that the child had been carried off while in her charge, and however hard it might be forher, few could blame the mother for wishing her removed from the house desolated by her lack of vigilance. But she was a good girl and felt the humiliation of her departure almost in the light of a disgrace.

As we came again into an open portion of the lawn, she stopped short and looked back.

"Oh!" she cried, gripping me by the arm, "there is Mrs. Ocumpaugh still at the window. All night she has stood there, except when she flew down to the river at the sound of some imaginary call from the boats. She believes, she really believes, that they will yet come upon Gwendolen's body in the dock there."

Following the direction of her glance, I looked up. Was that Mrs. Ocumpaugh—that haggard, intent figure with eyes fixed in awful expectancy on the sinister group I could picture to myself down at the water's edge? Never could I have imagined such a look on features I had always considered as cold as they were undeniably beautiful. As I took in the misery it expressed, that awful waiting for an event momently anticipated, and momently postponed, I found myself, without reason and simply in response to the force of her expression, unconsciously sharing her expectation, and with a momentary forgetfulness of all the probabilities, was about to turn toward the spot upon which her glances were fixed, when a touch on my arm recalled me to myself.

"Come!" whispered my trembling companion. "She may look down and see us here."

I yielded to her persuasion and turned away into the cluster of trees that lay between us and that opening in the hedge through which our course lay. Had I been alone I should not have budged till I had seen some change—any change—in the face whose appearance had so deeply affected me.

"Mrs. Ocumpaugh certainly believes that the body of her child lies in the water," I remarked, as we took our way onward as rapidly as possible. "Do you know her reasons for this?"

"She says, and I think she is right so far, that the child has been bent for a long time on fishing; that she has heard her father talk repeatedly of his great luck in Canada last year and wished to try the sport for herself; that she has been forbidden to go to the river, but must have taken the first opportunity when no eye was on her to do so; and — and — Mrs. Ocumpaugh shows a bit of string which she found last night in the bushes alongside the tracks when she ran down, as I have said, at some imaginary shout from the boats — a string which she declares she saw rolled up in Gwendolen's hand when she went into the bungalow to look at her. Of course, it may not be the same, but Mrs. Ocumpaugh thinks it is, and — "

"Do you think it possible, after all, that the child did stray down to the water?"

"No," was the vehement disclaimer. "Gwendolen's feet were excessively tender. She could not have taken three steps in only one shoe. I should have heard her cry out."

"What if she went in some one's arms?"

"A stranger's? She had a decided instinct against strangers. Never could any one she did not know and like have carried her so far as that without her waking. Then those men on the track, — they would have seen her. No, Mr. Trevitt, it was not inthatdirection she went."

The force of her emphasis convinced me that she had an opinion of her own in regard to this matter. Was it one she was ready to impart?

"In what direction, then?" I asked, with a gentleness I hoped would prove effective.

Her impulse was toward a frank reply. I saw her lips part and her eyes take on the look which precedes a direct avowal, but, as chance would have it, we came at that moment upon the thicket inclosing the bungalow, and the sight of its picturesque walls, showing brown through the verdure of the surrounding shrubbery, seemed to act as a check upon her, for, with a quick look and a certain dry accent quite new in her speech, she suddenly inquired if I did not want to see the place from which Gwendolen had disappeared.

Naturally I answered in the affirmative and followed her as she turned aside into the circular path which embraces this hidden retreat; but I had rather have heard her answer to my question, than to have gone anywhere or seen anything at that moment. Yet, when in full view of the bungalow's open door, she stopped to point out to me the nearness of the place to that opening in the hedge we had just been making for, and when she even went so far as to indicate the tangled little path by which that opening could be reached directly from the farther end of the bungalow, I considered that my question had been answered, though in another way than I anticipated, even before I noted the slight flush which rose to her cheek under my earnest scrutiny.

As it is important for the exact location of the bungalow to be understood, I subjoin a diagram of this part of the grounds:

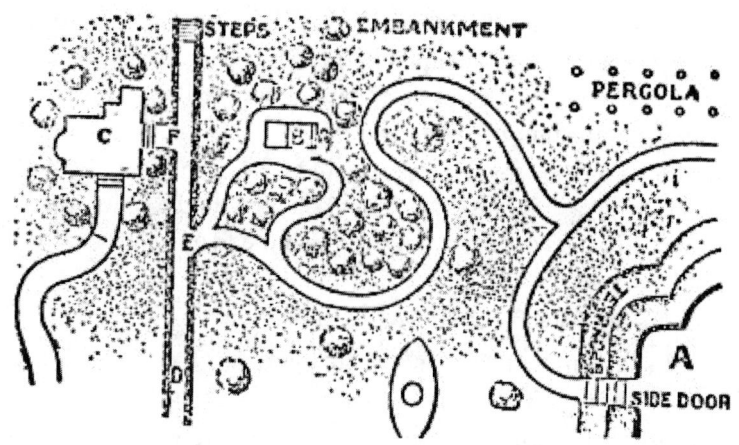

LAWN EXTENDING TO THE HIGHWAY.

A The Ocumpaugh mansion. B The Bungalow. C Mrs. Carew's house. D Private path. E Gap in hedge leading to the Ocumpaugh grounds. F Gap leading into Mrs. Carew's grounds. G Bench at end of bungalow.

As I took this all in, I ventured to ask some particulars of the family living so near the Ocumpaughs.

"Who occupies that house?" I asked, pointing to the sloping roofs and ornamental chimneys arising just beyond us over the hedge-rows.

"Oh, that is Mrs. Carew's home. She is a widow and Mrs. Ocumpaugh's dearest friend. How she loved Gwendolen! How we all loved her! And now, thatwretch—"

She burst into tears. They were genuine ones; so was her grief.

I waited till she was calm again, then I inquired very softly:

"What wretch?"

"You have not been inside," she suggested, pointing sharply to the bungalow.

I took the implied rebuke and entered the door she indicated. A man was sitting within, but he rose and went out when he saw us. He wore a policeman's badge and evidently recognized her or possibly myself. I noted, however, that he did not go far from the doorway.

"It is only a den," remarked Miss Graham.

I looked about me. She had described it perfectly: a place to lounge in on an August day like the present. Walls of Georgia pine across one of which

THE MILLIONAIRE BABY | 15

hung a series of long dark rugs; a long, low window looking toward the house, and a few articles of bamboo furniture describe the place. Among the latter was a couch. It was drawn up underneath the window, on the other side of which ran the bench where my companion declared she had been sitting while listening to the music.

"Wouldn't you think my attention would have been caught by the sound of any one moving about here?" she cried, pointing to the couch and then to the window. "But the window was closed and the door, as you see, is round the corner from the bench."

"A person with a very stealthy step, apparently."

"Very," she admitted. "Oh, how can I ever forgive myself! how can I ever, ever forgive myself!"

As she stood wringing her hands in sight of that empty couch, I cast a scrutinizing glance about me, which led me to remark:

"This interior looks new; much newer than the outside. It has quite a modern air."

"Yes, the bungalow is old, very old; but this room, or den, or whatever you might call it, was all remodeled and fitted up as you see it now when the new house went up. It had long been abandoned as a place of retreat, and had fallen into such decay that it was a perfect eyesore to all who saw it. Now it is likely to be abandoned again, and for what a reason! Oh, the dreadful place! How I hate it, now Gwendolen is gone!"

"One moment. I notice another thing. This room does not occupy the whole of the bungalow."

Either she did not hear me or thought it unnecessary to reply; and perceiving that her grief had now given way to an impatience to be gone, I did not press the matter, but led the way myself to the door. As we entered the little path which runs directly to that outlet in the hedge marked E, I ventured to speak again:

"You have reasons, or so it appears, for believing that the child was carried off through this very path?"

The reply was impetuous:

"How else could she have been spirited away so quickly? Besides,—" here her eye stole back at me over her shoulder,—"I have since remembered that as I ran out of the bungalow in my fright at finding the child gone, I heard the sound of wheels on Mrs. Carew's driveway. It did not mean much to me then, for I expected to find the child somewhere about the grounds; butnow, when I come to think, it means everything, for a child's cry mingled with it (or I imagined that it did) and that child —"

"But," I forcibly interposed, "the police should know this."

"They do; and so does Mrs. Ocumpaugh; but she has only the one idea, and nothing can move her."

I remembered the wagon with the crying child inside which had been seen on the roads the previous evening, and my heart fell a little in spite of myself.

"Couldn't Mrs. Carew tell us something about this?" I asked, with a gesture toward the house we were now passing.

"No. Mrs. Carew went to New York that morning and had only just returned when we missed Gwendolen. She had been for her little nephew, who has lately been made an orphan, and she was too busy making him feel at home to notice if a carriage had passed through her grounds."

"Her servants then?"

"She had none. All had been sent away. The house was quite empty."

I thought this rather odd, but having at this moment reached the long flight of steps leading down the embankment, I made no reply till we reached the foot. Then I observed:

"I thought Mrs. Carew was very intimate with Mrs. Ocumpaugh."

"She is; they are more like sisters than mere friends."

"Yet she goes to New York the very day her friend gives a musicale."

"Oh, she had good reasons for that. Mrs. Carew is planning to sail this week for Europe, and this was her only opportunity for getting her little nephew, who is to go with her. But I don't know as she will sail, now. She is wild with grief over Gwendolen's loss, and will not feel like leaving Mrs. Ocumpaugh till she knows whether we shall ever see the dear child again. But, I shall miss my train."

Here her step visibly hastened.

As it was really very nearly due, I had not the heart to detain her. But as I followed in her wake I noticed that for all her hurry a curious hesitancy crept into her step at times, and I should not have been surprised at any moment to see her stop and confront me on one of the two remaining long flights of steps leading down the steep hillside.

But we both reached the base without her having yielded to this impulse, and presently we found ourselves in full view of the river and the small flag-station located but a few rods away toward the left. As we turned toward the latter, we both cast an involuntary look back at the Ocumpaugh dock, where a dozen men could be seen at work dragging the river-bed with grappling irons. It made a sadly suggestive picture, and the young girl at my side shuddered violently as we noted the expression of morbid curiosity on the faces of such onlookers, men and women, as were drawn up at the end of the small point on which the boat-house stood.

But I had another reason than this for urging her on. I had noticed how, at the sight of her slight figure descending the slope, some half-dozen men or so had separated themselves from this group, with every appearance of intending to waylay and question her. She noticed this too, and drawing up more closely to my side, exclaimed with marked feeling:

"Save me from these men and I will tell you something that no one—"

But here she stopped, here our very thoughts stopped. A shout had risen from the group at the water-edge; a shout which made us both turn, and even caused the men who had started to follow us to wheel about and rush back to the dock with every appearance of intense excitement.

"What is it? What can it be?" faltered my greatly-alarmed companion.

"They have found something. See! what is that the man in the boat is holding up? It looks like—"

But she was already half-way to the point, outstripping the very men whose importunities she had shrunk from a moment before. I was not far behind her, and almost immediately we found ourselves wedged among the agitated group leaning over the little object which had been tossed ashore into the first hand outstretched to receive it.

It was a second little shoe—filled with sand and dripping with water, but recognizable as similar to the one already found on the preceding day high up on the bank. As this fact was borne in on us all, a groan of pity broke from more than one pair of lips, and eye after eye stole up the hillside to that far window in the great pile above us where the mother's form could be dimly discerned swaying in an agitation caught from our own excitement.

But there was one amongst us whose glance never left that little shoe. The train she had been so anxious to take whistled and went thundering by, but she never moved or noticed. Suddenly she reached out her hand.

"Let me see it, please," she entreated. "I was her nurse; let me take it in my hand."

The man who held it passed it over. She examined it long and closely.

"Yes, it is hers," said she. But in another moment she had laid it down with what I thought was a very peculiar look.

Instantly it was caught up and carried with a rush up the slope to where Mrs. Ocumpaugh could be seen awaiting it with outstretched arms. But I did not linger to mark her reception of it. Miss Graham had drawn me to one side and was whispering in my ear:

"I must talk to you. I can not keep back another moment what I think or what I feel. Some one is playing with Mrs. Ocumpaugh's fears. That shoe is Gwendolen's, but it is not the mate of the one found on the bank above. That was for the left footand so is this one. Did you not notice?"

II-"A FEARSOME MAN"

The effect of this statement upon me was greater than even she had contemplated.

"You thought the child had been stolen for the reward she would bring?" she continued. "She was not; she was taken out of pure hate, and that is why I suffer so. What may they not do to her! In what hole hide her! My darling, O my darling!"

She was going off into hysterics, but the look and touch I gave her recalled her to herself.

"We need to be calm," I urged. "You, because you have something of importance to impart, and I, because of the action I must take as soon as the facts you have concealed become known to me. What gives you such confidence in this belief, which I am sure is not shared by the police, and who is the some one who, as you say, is playing upon Mrs. Ocumpaugh's fears? A short time ago it was as the wretch you spoke of him. Are not some one and the wretch one and the same person, and can you not give him now a name?"

We had been moving all this time in the direction of the station and had now reached the foot of the platform. Pausing, she cast a last look up the bank. The trees were thick and hid from our view the Ocumpaugh mansion, but in imagination she beheld the mother moaning over that little shoe.

"I shall never return there," she muttered; "why do I hesitate so to speak!" Then in a burst, as I watched her in growing excitement: "She—Mrs. Ocumpaugh—begged me not to tell what she believed had nothing to do with our Gwendolen's loss. But I can not keep silence. This proof of a conspiracy against herself certainly relieves me from any promise I may have made her. Mr. Trevitt, I am positive that I know who carried off Gwendolen."

This was becoming interesting, intensely interesting to me. Glancing about and noting that the group down at the water-edge had become absorbed again in renewed efforts toward farther discoveries, I beckoned her to follow me into the station. It was but a step, but it gave me time to think. What was I encouraging this young girl to do? To reveal to me, who had no claim upon her but that of friendship, a secret which had not been given to the police? True, it might not be worth much, but it was also true that it might be worth a great deal. Did she know how much? I wanted money—few wanted it more—but I felt that I could not listen to her story till I had fairly settled this point. I therefore hastened to interpose a remark:

"Miss Graham, you are good enough to offer to reveal some fact hitherto concealed. Do you do this because you have no closer friend than myself, or because you do not know what such knowledge may be worth to the person you give it to—in money, I mean?"

"In money? I am not thinking of money," was her amazed reply; "I am thinking of Gwendolen."

"I understand, but you should think of the practical results as well. Have you not heard of the enormous reward offered by Mr. Ocumpaugh?"

"No; I—"

"Five thousand dollars for information; and fifty thousand to the one who will bring her back within the week unharmed. Mr. Ocumpaugh cabled to that effect yesterday."

"It is a large sum," she faltered, and for a moment she hesitated. Then, with a sweet and candid look which sank deep into my heart, she added gravely: "I had rather not think of money in connection with Gwendolen. If what I have to tell leads to her recovery, you can be trusted, I know, to do what is right toward me. Mr. Trevitt, the man who stole her from her couch and carried her away through Mrs. Carew's grounds in a wagon or otherwise, is a long-haired, heavily whiskered man of sixty or more years of age. His face is deeply wrinkled, but chiefly marked by a long scar running down between his eyebrows, which are so shaggy that they would quite hide his eyes if they were not lit up with an extraordinary expression of resolution, carried almost to the point of frenzy; a fearsome man, making your heart stand still when he pauses to speak to you."

Startled as I had seldom been, for reasons which will hereafter appear, I surveyed her in mingled wonder and satisfaction.

"His name?" I demanded.

"I do not know his name."

Again I stopped to look at her.

"Does Mrs. Ocumpaugh?"

"I do not think so. She only knows what I told her."

"And what did you tell her?"

"Ah! who are these?"

Two or three persons had entered the station, probably to wait for the next train.

"No one who will molest you."

But she was not content till we had withdrawn to where the time-table hung up on the opposite wall. Turning about as if to consult it, she told the following story. I never see a time-table now but I think of her expression as she stood there looking up as if her mind were fixed on what she probably did not see at all.

"Last Wednesday—no, it was on the Wednesday preceding—I was taking a ride with Gwendolen on one of the side roads branching off toward Fordham. We were in her own little pony cart, and as we seldom rode together like this, she had been chattering about a hundred things till her eyes danced in her head and she looked as lovely as I had ever seen her. But suddenly, just as we were about to cross a small wooden bridge, I saw her turn pale and her whole sensitive form quiver. 'Some one I don't like,' she cried. 'There is some one about whom I don't like. Drive on, Ellie, drive on.' But before I could gather up the reins a figure which I had not noticed before stepped from behind a tree at the farther end of the bridge, and advancing into the middle of the road with arms thrown out, stopped our advance. I have told you how he looked, but I can give you no idea of the passionate fury lighting up his eyes, or the fiery dignity with which he held his place and kept us subdued to his will till he had looked the shrinking child all over, and laughed, not as a madman laughs, oh, much too slow and ironically for that! but like one who takes an unholy pleasure in mocking the happy present with evil prophecy. Nothing that I can say will make you see him as I saw him in that one instant, and though there was much in the circumstance to cause fear, I think it was more awe than fright we felt, so commanding was his whole appearance and so forcible the assurance with which he held us there till he was ready to move. Gwendolen cried out, but the imploring sound had no effect upon him; it only reawakened his mirth and led him to say, in a clear, cold, mocking tone which I hear yet, 'Cry out, little one, for your short day is nearly over. Silks and feathers and carriages and servants will soon be a half-forgotten memory to you; and right it is that it should be so. Ten days, little one, only ten days more.' And with that he moved, and, slipping aside behind the tree, allowed us to drive on. Mr. Trevitt, yesterday saw the end of those ten days, and where is she now? Only that man knows. He is one man in a thousand. Can not you find him?"

She turned; a train was coming, a train which it was very evident she felt it her duty to take. I had no right to detain her, but I found time for a question or two.

"And you told Mrs. Ocumpaugh this?"

"The moment we arrived home."

"And she? What did she think of it?"

"Mrs. Ocumpaugh is not a talkative woman. She grew very white and clasped the child passionately in her arms. But the next minute she had to all appearance dismissed the whole occurrence from her thoughts. 'Some socialistic fanatic,' she called him and merely advised me to stop driving with Gwendolen for the present."

"Didn't you recall the matter to her when you found the child missing?"

"Yes; but then she appeared to regard it in a superstitious way only. It was a warning of death, she said, and the man an irresponsible clairvoyant. When I tried to urge my own idea upon her and describe how I thought he might have obtained access to the bungalow and carried her off, while still asleep, to some vehicle awaiting them in Mrs. Carew's grounds, she only rebuked me for my folly and bade me keep still about the whole occurrence, saying that I should only be getting some poor half-demented old wretch into trouble for something for which he was not in the least responsible."

"A very considerate woman," I remarked; to which Miss Graham made reply as the train came storming up:

"Nobody knows how considerate, even if she has dismissed me rather suddenly from her service. Don't let that wretch"—again she used the word—"deceive her or you into thinking that the little one perished in the water. Gwendolen is alive, I say. Find him and you will find her. I saw his resolution in his eye."

Here she made a rush for the cars, and I had time only to get her future address before the train started and all further opportunity of conversation between us was over for that day.

I remained behind because I was by no means through with my investigations. What she had told me only convinced me of the necessity I had already recognized of making myself master of all that could be learned at Homewood before undertaking the very serious business of locating the child or even the aged man just described to me, and who I was now sure had been the chief, if not the sole, instrument in her abduction.

III-A CHARMING WOMAN

Stopping only long enough to send a telegram to my partner in New York, (for which purpose I had to walk along the tracks to the main station) I returned by the short cut to Homewood. My purpose in doing this was twofold. I should have a chance of seeing if the men were still at work in the river, and I should also have the added opportunity of quietly revisiting the bungalow, on the floor of which I had noted some chalk-marks, which I felt called for a closer examination than I had given them. As I came in view of the dock, I saw that the men were still busy, but at a point farther out in the river, as if all hope had been abandoned of their discovering anything more inshore. But the chalk-marks in the bungalow were almost forgotten by me in the interest I experienced in a certain adventure which befell me on my way there.

I had just reached the opening in the hedge communicating with Mrs. Carew's grounds, when I heard steps on the walk inside and a woman's rich voice saying:

"There, that will do. You must play on the other side of the house, Harry. And Dinah, see that he does so, and that he does not cross the hall again till I come back. The sight of so merry a child might kill Mrs. Ocumpaugh if she happened to look this way."

Moved by the tone, which was one in a thousand, I involuntarily peered through the outlet I was passing, in the hope of catching a glimpse of its owner, and thus was favored with the sight of a face which instantly fixed itself in my memory as one of the most enchanting I had ever encountered. Not from its beauty, yet it may have been beautiful; nor from its youth, for the woman before me was not youthful, but from the extraordinary eloquence of its expression caught at a rare moment when the heart, which gave it life, was full. She was standing half-way down the path, throwing kisses to a little boy who was leaning toward her from an upper window. The child was laughing with glee, and it was this laugh she was trying to check; but her countenance, as she made the effort, was almost as merry as his, and yet was filled with such solemn joy—such ecstasy of motherhood I should be inclined to call it, if I had not been conscious that this must be Mrs. Carew and the child her little nephew — that in my admiration for this exhibition of pure feeling, I forgot to move on as she advanced into the hedge-row, and so we came face to face. The result was as extraordinary to me as all the rest. Instantly all the gay abandonment left her features, and she showed me a grave, almost troubled, countenance, more in keeping with her severe dress, which was as nearly like mourning as it could be and not be made of crape.

It was such a sudden change and of so complete a character, that I was thrown off my guard for a moment and probably betrayed the curiosity I undoubtedly felt; for she paused as she reached me, and, surveying me very quietly but very scrutinizingly too, raised again that marvelous voice of hers and pointedly observed:

"This is a private path, sir. Only the friends of Mrs. Ocumpaugh or of myself pass here."

This was a speech calculated to restore my self-possession. With a bow which evidently surprised her, I answered with just enough respect to temper my apparent presumption:

"I am here in the interests of Mrs. Ocumpaugh, to assist her in finding her child. Moments are precious; so I ventured to approach by the shorter way."

"Pardon me!" The words did not come instantly, but after some hesitation, during which she kept her eyes on my face in a way to rob me of all thought save that she possessed a very strong magnetic quality, to which it were well for a man like myself to yield. "You will be my friend, too, if you succeed in restoring Gwendolen." Then quickly, as she crossed to the Ocumpaugh grounds: "You do not look like a member of the police. Are you here at Mrs. Ocumpaugh's bidding, and has she at last given up all expectation of finding her child in the river?"

I, too, thought a minute before answering, then I put on my most candid expression, for was not this woman on her way to Mrs. Ocumpaugh, and would she not be likely to repeat what she heard me say?

"I do not know how Mrs. Ocumpaugh feels at present. But I know what her dearest wish is — to see her child again alive and well. That wish I shall do my best to gratify. It is true that I am not a police detective, but I have an agency of my own, well-known to both Mrs. and Mr. Ocumpaugh. All its resources will be devoted to this business and I hope to succeed, madam. If, as I suspect, you are on your way to Mrs. Ocumpaugh, please tell her that Robert Trevitt, of Trevitt and Jupp, hopes to succeed."

"I will," she emphasized. Then stepping back to me in all the grace of her thrilling personality, she eagerly added: "If there is any information I can give, do not be afraid to ask me. I love children, and would give anything in the world to see Mrs. Ocumpaugh as happy with Gwendolen again as I am with my little nephew. Are you quite sure that there is any possibility of this? I was told that the child's shoe has been found in the river; but almost immediately following this information came the report that there was something odd about this shoe, and that Mrs. Ocumpaugh had gone into hysterics. Doyouknow what they meant by that? I was just going over to see."

I did know what they meant, but I preferred to seem ignorant.

"I have not seen Mrs. Ocumpaugh," I evasively rejoined. "ButIdon't look for the child to be drawn from the water."

"Nor I," she repeated, with a hoarse catch in her breath. "It is thirty-six hours since we lost her. Time enough for the current to have carried her sweet little body far away from here."

I surveyed the lady before me in amazement.

"Thenyouthink she strayed down to the water?"

"Yes; it would madden me to believe otherwise; loving her so well, and her parents so well, I dare not think of a worse fate."

Taking advantage of her amiability and the unexpected opportunity it offered for a leading question, I hereupon ventured to say: "You were not at home, I hear, when she vanished from the bungalow."

"No; that is, if it happened before three o'clock. I arrived from the station just as the clock was striking the hour, and having my little nephew with me, I was too much occupied in reconciling him to his new home, to hear or see anything outside. Most unfortunate!" she mourned, "most unfortunate! I shall never cease reproaching myself. A tragedy at my door" — here she glanced across the shrubbery at the bungalow — "and I occupied with my own affairs!"

With a flush, the undoubted result of her own earnestness, she turned as if to go. But I could not let her depart without another question:

"Excuse me, Mrs. Carew, but you gave me permission to seem importunate. With the exception of her nurse, you were the one person nearest the bungalow at the time. Didn't you hear a carriage drive through your grounds at about the hour the alarm was first started? I know you have been asked this before, but not by me; and it is a very important fact to have settled; very important for those who wish to discover this child at once."

For reply she gave me a look of very honest amazement.

"Of course I did," she replied. "I came in a carriage myself from the station and naturally heard it drive away."

At her look, at her word, the thread which I had seized with such avidity seemed to slip from my fingers. Had little Miss Graham's theory no better foundation than this? and were the wheels she heard only those of Mrs. Carew's departing carriage? I resolved to press the matter even if I ran the risk of displeasing her.

"Mrs. Carew—for it must be Mrs. Carew I am addressing—did your little nephew cry when you first brought him to the house?"

"I think he did," she admitted slowly; "I think he did."

I must have given evidence of the sudden discouragement this brought me, for her lips parted and her whole frame trembled with sudden earnestness.

"Did you think—did any one think—that those cries came from Gwendolen? That she was carried out through my grounds? Could any one have thought that?"

"I have been told that the nursery-governess did."

"Little Miss Graham? Poor girl! she is but defending herself from despair. She is ready to believe everything but that the child is dead."

Was it so? Was I following the false light of a will-o'-the-wisp? No, no; the strange coincidence of the threat made on the bridge with the disappearance of the child on the day named, was at least real. The thread had not altogether escaped from my hands. It was less tangible, but it was still there.

"You may be right," I acquiesced, for I saw that her theories were entirely opposed to those of Miss Graham. "But we must try everything,everything."

I was about to ask whether she had ever seen in the adjoining grounds, or on the roads about, an old man with long hair and a remarkable scar running down between his eyebrows, when a young girl in the cap and apron of a maid-servant came running through the shrubbery from the Ocumpaugh house, and, seeing Mrs. Carew, panted out:

"Oh, do come over to the house, Mrs. Carew. Mrs. Ocumpaugh has been told that the two shoes which have been found, one on the bank and the other in the river, are not mates, and it has quite distracted her. She has gone to her room and will let no one else in. We can hear her moaning and crying, but we can do nothing. Perhaps she will see you. She called for you, I know, before she shut her door."

"I will go." Mrs. Carew had turned quite pale, and from standing upright in the road, had moved so as to gain support from one of the hedges.

I expected to see her turn and go as soon as her trembling fit was over, but she did not, though she waved the girl away as if she intended to follow her. Had I not learned to distrust my own impression of people's motives from their manners and conduct, I should have said that she was waiting for me to precede her.

"Two shoes and not mates!" she finally exclaimed. "What does she mean?"

"Simply that another shoe has been drawn up from the river-bottom which does not mate the one picked up near the bungalow. Both are for the left foot."

"Ah!" gasped this sympathetic woman. "And what inference can we draw from that?"

I should not have answered her; but the command in her eyes or the thrilling effect of her manner compelled me, and I spoke the truth at once, just as I might have done to Mrs. Ocumpaugh, or, better still, to Mr. Ocumpaugh, if either had insisted.

"But one," said I. "There is a conspiracy on the part of one or more persons to delude Mrs. Ocumpaugh into believing the child dead. They blundered over it, but they came very near succeeding."

"Who blundered, and what is the meaning of the conspiracy you hint at? Tell me. Tell me what such men as you think."

Her plastic features had again shown a change. She was all anxiety now; cheeks burning, eyes blazing—a very beautiful woman.

"We think that the case looks serious. We think from the very mystery it displays, that there is a keen intelligence back of this crime. I can not go any further than that. The affair is as yet too obscure."

"You amaze me!" she faltered, making an effort to collect her thoughts. "I have always thought, just as Mrs. Ocumpaugh has, that the child had somehow found her way to the water and was drowned. But if all this is true we shall have to face a worse evil. A conspiracy against such a tender little being as that! A conspiracy, and for what? Not to extort money, or why these blundering efforts to make the child appear dead?"

She was the same sympathetic woman, agitated by real feeling as before, yet at this moment—I do not understand now just why—I became aware of an inner movement of caution against too great a display of candor on my own part.

"Madam, it is all a mystery at present. I am sure that the police will tell you the same. But another day may bring developments."

"Let us hope so!" was her ardent reply, accompanied by a gesture, the freedom of which suited her style and person as it would not have done those of a less impressionable woman. And, seeing that I had no intention of leaving the spot where I stood, she moved at last from where she held herself upright against the hedge, and entered the Ocumpaugh grounds. "Will you call in to see me to-morrow?" she asked, pausing to look back at a turn in the path. "I shall not sleep to-night for thinking of those possible developments."

"Since you permit me," I returned; "that is, if I am still here. Affairs may call me away at any moment."

"Yes, and so with me. Affairs may call me away also. I was to sail on Saturday for Liverpool. Only Mrs. Ocumpaugh's distress detains me. If the situation lightens, if we hear any good news to-night, or even early to-morrow, I shall continue my preparations, which will take me again to New York."

"I will call if you are at home."

She gave me a slight nod and vanished.

Why did I stand a good three minutes where she had left me, thinking, but not getting anything from my thoughts, save that I was glad that I had not been betrayed into speaking of the old man Miss Graham had met on the bridge? Yet it might have been well, after all, if I had done so, if only to discover whether Mrs. Ocumpaugh had confided this occurrence to her most intimate friend.

IV-CHALK-MARKS

My next move was toward the bungalow. Those chalk-marks still struck me as being worthy of investigation, and not only they, but the bungalow itself. That certainly merited a much closer inspection than I had been able to give it under Miss Graham's eye.

It was not quite a new place to me, nor was I so ignorant of its history (and it had a history) as I had appeared to be in my conversation with Miss Graham. Originally it had been a stabling place for horses; and tradition said that it had once harbored for a week the horse of General Washington. This was when the house on the knoll above had been the seat and home of one of our most famous Revolutionary generals. Later, as the trees grew up around this building, it attracted the attention of a new owner, William Ocumpaugh, the first of that name to inhabit Homewood, and he, being a man of reserved manners and very studious habits, turned it into what we would now call, as Miss Graham did, a den, but which he styled a pavilion, and used as a sort of study or reading-room.

His son, who inherited it, Judge Philo Ocumpaugh, grandfather of the present Philo, was as studious as his father, but preferred to read and write in the quaint old library up at the house, famous for its wide glass doors opening on to the lawn, and its magnificent view of the Hudson. His desk, which many remember (it has a place in the present house, I believe), was so located that for forty years or more he had this prospect ever before him, a prospect which included the sight of his own pavilion, around which, for no cause apparent to his contemporaries, he had caused a high wall to be built, effectually shutting in both trees and building.

This wall has since been removed; but I have often heard it spoken of, and always with a certain air of mystery; possibly because, as I have said, there seemed no good reason for its erection, the place holding no treasure and the gate standing always open; possibly because of its having been painted, in defiance of all harmony with everything about the place, a dazzling white; and possibly because it had not been raised till after the death of the judge's first wife, who, some have said, breathed her last within the precincts it inclosed.

However that may be, there seems to be no doubt that this place exerted, very likely against his will, for he never visited it, a singular fascination over the secretive mind of this same upright but strangely taciturn ancestor of the Ocumpaughs. For during the forty years in which he wrote and read at this desk, the shutters guarding the door overlooking those decaying walls were never drawn to, or so the tradition runs; and when he died, it was found that, by a clause in his will, this pavilion, hut or bungalow, all of which names it bore at different stages of its existence, was recommended to the notice of his heirs as an object which they were at liberty to leave in its present forsaken condition, though he did not exact this, but which was never, under any circumstances or to serve any purpose, to be removed from its present site, or even to suffer any demolition save such as came with time and the natural round of the seasons, to whose tender mercies he advised it to be left. In other words, it was to stand, and to stand unmolested, till it fell of its own accord, or was struck to the earth by lightning—a tragic alternative in the judgment of those who knew it for a structure of comparative insignificance, and one which, in the minds of many, and perhaps I may say in my own, appeared to point to some serious and unrevealed cause not unlinked with the almost forgotten death of that young wife to which I have just alluded.

This was years ago, far back in the fifties, and his son, who was a minor at his death, grew up and assumed his natural proprietorship. The hut—it was nothing but a hut now—had remained untouched—a ruin no longer habitable. The spirit, as well as the letter, of that particular clause in his father's will had so far been literally obeyed. The walls being of stone, had withstood decay, and still rose straight and firm; but the roof had begun to sag, and whatever of woodwork yet remained about it had rotted and fallen away, till the building was little more than a skeleton, with holes for its windows and an open gap for its door.

As for the surrounding wall, it no longer stood out, an incongruous landmark, from its background of trees and shrubbery. Young shoots had started up and old branches developed till brick and paint alike were almost concealed from view by a fresh girdle of greenery.

And now comes the second mystery.

Sometime after this latter Ocumpaugh had attained his majority—his name was Edwin, and he was, as you already imagine, the father of the present Philo—he made an attempt—a daring one it was afterward called—to brighten this neglected spot and restore it to some sort of use, by giving a supper to his friends within its broken-down walls.

This supper was no orgy, nor were the proprieties in any way transgressed by so harmless a festivity; yet from this night a singular change was observed in this man. Pleasure no longer charmed him, and instead of repeating the experiment I have just described, he speedily evinced such an antipathy to the scene of his late revel that only from the greatest necessity would he ever again visit that part of the grounds.

What did it mean? What had occurred on that night of innocent enjoyment to disturb or alarm him? Had some note in his own conscience been struck by an act which, in his cooler moments, he may have looked upon as a species of sacrilege? Or had some whisper from the past reached him amid the feasting, the laughing and the jesting, to render these old walls henceforth intolerable to him? He never said, but whatever the cause of this sudden aversion, the effect was deep and promised to be lasting. For, one morning, not long after this event, a party of workmen was seen leaving these grounds at daybreak, and soon it was noised about that a massive brick partition had been put up across the interior of this same pavilion, completely shutting off, for no reason that any one could see, some ten feet of what had been one long and undivided room.

It was a strange act enough; but when, a few days later, it was followed by one equally mysterious, and they saw the encircling wall which had been so carefully raised by Judge Ocumpaugh ruthlessly pulled down, and every sign of its former presence there destroyed, wonder filled the highway and the curiosity of neighbors and friends passed all bounds.

But no explanations were volunteered then or ever. People might query and peer, but they learned nothing. What was left open to view told no tales beyond the old one, and as for the single window which was the sole opening into the shut-off space, it was then, as now, so completely blocked up by a network of closely impacted vines, that it offered little more encouragement than the wall itself to the eyes of such curiosity-mongers as crept in by way of the hedge-rows to steal a look at the hut, and if possible gain a glimpse of an interior which had suddenly acquired, by the very means taken to shut it off from every human eye, a new importance pointing very decidedly toward the tragic.

But soon even this semblance of interest died out or was confined to strange tales whispered under breath on weird nights at neighboring firesides, and the old neglect prevailed once more. The whole place—new brick and old stone—seemed doomed to a common fate under the hand of time, when the present Philo Ocumpaugh, succeeding to the property, brought new wealth and business enterprise into the family, and the old house on the hill was replaced by the marble turrets of Homewood, and this hut—or rather the portion open to improvement—was restored to some sort of comfort, and rechristened the bungalow.

Was fate to be appeased by this effort at forgetfulness? No. In emulation of the long abandoned portion so hopelessly cut off by that dividing wall, this brightly-furnished adjunct to the great house had linked itself in the minds of men to a new mystery—the mystery which I had come there to solve, if wit and patience could do it, aided by my supposedly unshared knowledge of a fact connecting me with this family's history in a way it little dreamed of.

Naturally, my first look was at the building itself. I have described its location and the room from which the child was lost. What I wanted to see now, after studying those chalk-marks, was whether that partition which had been put in, was as impassable as was supposed.

The policeman on guard having strolled a few feet away, I approached the open doorway without hindrance, and at once took that close look I had promised myself, of the marks which I had observed scrawled broadly across the floor just inside the threshold. They were as interesting and fully as important as I had anticipated. Though nearly obliterated by the passing of the policeman's feet across them, I was still enabled to read the one word which appeared to me significant.

If you will glance at the following reproduction of a snap-shot which I took of this scrawl, you will see what I mean.

$$\mathcal{U}s\!\!\!\mathrel{\vrule height 1.4ex}\ \ 16\ \ \mathrel{\vrule height 1.4ex}\!\!\!\mathcal{}$$

The significant character was the 16. Taken with the "ust," there could be no doubt that the whole writing had been a record of the date on which the child had disappeared: August 16, 190-.

This in itself was of small consequence if the handwriting had not possessed those marked peculiarities which I believed belonged to but one man—a man I had once known—a man of reverend aspect, upright carriage and a strong distinguishing mark, like an old-time scar, running straight down between his eyebrows. This had been my thought when I first saw it. It was doubly so on seeing it again after the doubts expressed by Miss Graham of a threatening old man who possessed similar characteristics.

Satisfied on this point, I turned my attention to what still more seriously occupied it. The three or four long rugs, which hung from the ceiling across the whole wall at my left, evidently concealed the mysterious partition put up in Mr. Ocumpaugh's father's time directly across this portion of the room. Was it a totally unbroken partition? I had been told so; but I never accept such assertions without a personal investigation.

Casting a glance through the doorway and seeing that it would take my dreaming friend, the policeman, some two or three minutes yet to find his way back to his post, I hastily lifted these rugs aside, one after the other, and took a look behind them. A stretch of Georgia pine, laid, as I readily discovered by more than one rap of my knuckles, directly over the bricks it was intended to conceal, was visible under each; from end to end a plain partition with no indications of its having been tampered with since the alterations were first made.

Dismissing from my mind one of those vague possibilities, which add such interest to the calling of a detective, I left the place, with my full thought concentrated on the definite clue I had received from the chalk-marks.

But I had not walked far before I met with a surprise which possibly possessed a significance equal to anything I had already observed, if only I could have fully understood it.

On the path into which I now entered, I encountered again the figure of Mrs. Carew. Her face was turned full on mine, and she had evidently retraced her steps to have another instant's conversation with me. The next moment I was sure of this. Her eyes, always magnetic, shone with increasing brightness as I advanced to meet her, and her manner, while grave, was that of a woman quite conscious of the effect she produced by her least word or action.

"I have returned to tell you," said she, "that I have more confidence in your efforts than in those of the police officers around here. If Gwendolen's fate is determined by any one it will be by you. So I want to be of aid to you if I can. Remember that. I may have said this to you before, but I wish to impress it upon you."

There was a flutter in her movements which astonished me. She was surveying me in a straightforward way, and I could not but feel the fire and force of her look. Happily she was no longer a young woman or I might have misunderstood the disturbance which took place in my own breast as I waited for the musical tones to cease.

"You are very good," I rejoined. "I need help, and shall be only too glad to receive your assistance."

Yet I did question her, though I presently found myself walking toward the house at her side. She may not have expected me to presume so far. Certainly she showed no dissatisfaction when, at a parting in the path, I took my leave of her and turned my face in the direction of the gates. A strange sweet woman, with a power quite apart from the physical charms which usually affect men of my age, but one not easily read nor parted from unless one had an imperative errand, as I had.

This errand was to meet and forestall the messenger boy whom I momently expected with the answer to my telegram. That an opportunity for gossip was likewise afforded by the motley group of men and boys drawn up near one of the gate-posts, gave an added interest to the event which I was quite ready to appreciate. Approaching this group, I assimilated myself with it as speedily as possible, and, having some tact for this sort of thing, soon found myself the recipient of various gratuitous opinions as to the significance of the find which had offered such a problem both to the professional and unprofessional detective. Two mismated shoes! Had Gwendolen Ocumpaugh by any chance worn such? No—or the ones mating them would have been found in her closet, and this, some one shouted out, had not been done. Only the one corresponding to that fished up from the waters of the dock had come to light; the other, the one which the child must really have worn, was no nearer being found than the child herself. What did it all mean? No one knew; but all attempted some sort of hazardous guess which I was happy to see fell entirely short of the mark.

There was not a word of the vindictive old man described by Miss Graham, till I myself introduced the topic. My reason or rather my excuse for introducing it was this:

On the gate-post near me I had observed the remnants of a strip of paper which had been pasted there and afterward imperfectly torn off. It had an unsightly look, but I did not pay much attention to it till some movement in the group forced me a little nearer to the post, when I was surprised enough to see that this scrap of paper showed signs of words, and that these words gave evidence of being a date written in the very hand I now had no difficulty in recognizing as that of the old man uppermost in my own mind, even if he were not the one whom Miss Graham had seen on the bridge. This date— strange to say—was the same significant one already noted on the floor of the bungalow—a fact which I felt merited an explanation if any one about me could give it.

Waiting, therefore, for a lull in the remarks passing between the stable-men and other employees about the place, I drew the attention of the first man who would listen, to the half torn-off strip of paper on the post, and asked if that was the way the Ocumpaughs gave notice of their entertainments.

He started, then turned his back on me.

"That wasn't put there for the entertainment," he growled; "that was pasted up there by some one who wanted to show off his writin'. There don't seem to be no other reason."

As the man who spoke these words had thereby proved himself a blockhead, I edged away from him as soon as possible toward a very decent looking fellow who appeared to have more brains than speech.

"Do you know who pasted that date upon the post?" I inquired.

He answered very directly.

"No, or I should have been laying for him long before this. Why, it is not only there you can see it. I found it pinned to the carriage cushions one day just as I was going to drive Mrs. Ocumpaugh out." (Evidently I had struck upon the coachman.) "And not only that. One of the girls up at the house—one as I knows pretty well—tells me—I don't care who hears it now—that it was written across a card which was left at the door for Mrs. Ocumpaugh, and all in the same handwriting, which is not a common one, as you can see. This means something, seeing it was the date when our bad luck fell on us."

He had noted that.

"You don't mean to say that these things were written and put about before the date you see on them."

"But I do. Would we have noticed since? But who are you, sir, if I may ask? One of them detective fellows? If so, I have a word to say: Find that child or Mrs. Ocumpaugh's blood will be on your head! She'll not live till Mr. Ocumpaugh comes home unless she can show him his child."

"Wait!" I called out, for he was turning away toward the stable. "You know who wrote those slips?"

"Not a bit of it. No one does. Not that anybody thinks much about them but me."

"The police must," I ventured.

"May be, but they don't say anything about it. Somehow it looks to me as if they were all at sea."

"Possibly they are," I remarked, letting him go as I caught sight of a small boy coming up the road with several telegrams in his hand.

"Is one of those directed to Robert Trevitt?" I asked, crowding up with the rest, as his small form was allowed to slip through the gate.

"Spec's there is," he replied, looking them over and handing me one.

I carried it to one side and hastily tore it open. It was, as I expected, from my partner, and read as follows:

Man you want has just returned after two days' absence. Am on watch. Saw him just alight from buggy with what looked like sleeping child in his arms. Closed and fastened front door after him. Safe for to-night.

Did I allow my triumph to betray itself? I do not think so. The question which kept down my elation was this: Would I be the first man to get there?

V-THE OLD HOUSE IN YONKERS

The old man whose handwriting I had now positively identified was a former employer of mine. I had worked in his office when a lad. He was a doctor of very fair reputation in Westchester County, and I recognized every characteristic of his as mentioned by Miss Graham, save the frenzy which she described as accompanying his address.

In those days he was calm and cold and, while outwardly scrupulous, capable of forgetting his honor as a physician under a sufficiently strong temptation. I had left him when new prospects opened, and in the years which had elapsed had contented myself with the knowledge that his shingle still hung out in Yonkers, though his practice was nothing to what it used to be when I was in his employ. Now I was going to see him again.

That his was the hand which had stolen Gwendolen seemed no longer open to doubt. That she was under his care in the curious old house I remembered in the heart of Yonkers, seemed equally probable; but why so sordid a man — one who loved money above everything else in the world — should retain the child one minute after the publication of the bountiful reward offered by Mr. Ocumpaugh, was what I could not at first understand. Miss Graham's theory of hate had made no impression on me. He was heartless and not likely to be turned aside from any project he had formed, but he was not what I considered vindictive where nothing was to be gained. Yet my comprehension of him had been but a boy's comprehension, and I was now prepared to put a very different estimate on one whose character had never struck me as being an open one, even when my own had been most credulous.

That my enterprise, even with the knowledge I possessed of this man, promised well or held out any prospects of easy fulfilment, I no longer allowed myself to think. If money was his object — and what other could influence a man of his temperament? — the sum offered by Mr. Ocumpaugh, large though it was, had apparently not sufficed to satisfy his greed. He was holding back the child, or so I now believed, in order to wring a larger, possibly a double, amount from the wretched mother. Fifty thousand was a goodly sum, but one hundred thousand was better; and this man had gigantic ideas where his cupidity was concerned. I remember how firmly he had once stood out for ten thousand dollars when he had been offered five; and I began to see, though in an obscure way as yet, how it might very easily be a part of his plan to work Mrs. Ocumpaugh up to a positive belief in the child's death before he came down upon her for the immense reward he had fixed his heart upon. The date he had written all over the place might thus find some explanation in a plan to weaken her nerve before pressing his exorbitant claims upon her.

Nothing was clear, yet everything was possible in such a nature; and anxious to enter upon the struggle both for my own sake and that of the child of whose condition under that terrible eye I scarcely dared to think, I left Homewood in haste and took the first train for Yonkers. Though the distance was not great, I had fully arranged my plans before entering the town where so many of my boyish years had been spent. I knew the old fox well enough, or thought I did, to be certain that I should have anything but an easy entrance into his house, in case it still harbored the child whom my partner had seen carried in there. I anticipated difficulties, but was concerned about none but the possibility of not being able to bring myself face to face with him. Once in his presence, the knowledge which I secretly possessed of an old but doubtful transaction of his, would serve to make him mine even to the point of yielding up the child he had forcibly abducted. But would he accord me an interview? Could I, without appeal to the police—and you can readily believe I was not anxious to allow them to put their fingers in my pie—force him to open his door and let me into his house, which, as I well recalled, he locked up at nine—after which he would receive no one, not even a patient?

It was not nine yet, but it was very near that hour. I had but twenty minutes in which to mount the hill to the old house marked by the doctor's sign and by another peculiarity of so distinct a nature that it would serve to characterize a dwelling in a city as large as New York—though I doubt if New York can show its like from the Battery to the Bronx. The particulars of this I will mention later. I have first to relate the relief I felt when, on entering the old neighborhood, I heard in response to a few notes of a certain popular melody which I had allowed to leave my lips, an added note or two which warned me that my partner was somewhere hidden among the alleys of this very unaristocratic quarter. Indeed, from the sound, I judged him to be in the rear of the doctor's house and, being anxious to hear what he had to say before advancing upon the door which might open my way to easy fortune or complete defeat, I paused a few steps off and waited for his appearance.

He was at my elbow before I had either seen or heard him. He was always light of foot, but this time he seemed to have no tread at all.

"Still here," was his comforting assurance.

"Both?" I whispered back.

"Both."

"Any one else?"

"No. A boy drove away the buggy and has not come back. Sawbones keeps no girl."

"Is the child quiet? Has there been no alarm?"

"Not a breath."

"No cops in the neighborhood? No spies around?"

"Not one. We've got it all this time. But—"

"Hush!"

"There's nobody."

"Yes, the doctor; he's fastening up his house. I must hasten; nothing would induce me to let that innocent remain under his roof all night."

"It's not the windows he is at."

"What then?"

"The door, the big front door."

"The—"

"Yes."

I gave my partner a surprised look, undoubtedly lost in the darkness, and drew a step nearer the house.

"It's just the same old gloom-box," I exclaimed, and paused for an instant to mark the changes which had taken place in the surroundings. They were very few and I turned back to fix my eye on the front door where a rattling sound could be heard, as of some one fingering the latch. It was this door which formed the peculiarity of the house. In itself it was like any other that was well-fashioned and solid, but it opened upon space—that is, if it was ever opened, which I doubted. The stoop and even the railing which had once guarded it, had all been removed, leaving a bare front, with this inhospitable entrance shut against every one who had not the convenience for mounting to it by a ladder. There was another way in, but this was round on one side, and did not present itself to the eye unless one approached from the west end of the street; so that to half the passers-by the house looked like a deserted one till they came abreast of the flagged path which led to the office door. As the windows had never been unclosed in my day and were not now, I took it for granted that they had remained thus inhospitably shut during all the years of my absence, which certainly offered but little encouragement to a man bent on an errand which would soon take him into those dismal precincts.

"What goes on behind those shuttered windows?" thought I. "I know of one thing, but what else?" The one thing was the counting of money and the arranging of innumerable gold pieces on the great top of a baize-covered table in what I should now describe as the back parlor. I remembered how he used to do it. I caught him at it once, having crept up one windy night from my little room off the office to see what kept the doctor up so late.

As I now stood listening in the dark street to those strange touches on a door disused for years, I recalled the tremor with which I rounded the top of the stair that night of long ago and the mingled fear and awe with which I recognized, not only such a mint of money as I had never seen out of the bank before, but the greedy and devouring passion with which he pushed the glittering coins about and handled the bank-notes and gloated over the pile it all made when drawn together by his hooked fingers, till the sound, perhaps, of my breathing in the dark hall startled him with a thought of discovery, and his two hands came together over that pile with a gesture more eloquent even than the look with which he seemed to penetrate the very shadows in the silent space wherein I stood. It was a vision short, but inexpressibly vivid, of the miser incarnate, and having seen it and escaped detection, as was my undeserved luck that night, I needed never to ask again why he had been willing to accept risks from which most men shrink from fear if not from conscience. He loved money, not as the spender loves it, openly and with luxurious instincts, but secretly and with a knavish dread of discovery which spoke of treasure ill acquired.

And now he was seeking to add to his gains, and I stood on the outside of his house listening to sounds I did not understand, instead of attempting to draw him to the office-door by ringing the bell he never used to disconnect till nine.

"Do you know that I don't quite like the noises which are being made up there?" came in a sudden whisper to my ear. "Supposing it was the child trying to get out! She does not know there is no stoop; she seemed sleeping or half-dead when he carried her in, and if by any chance she has got hold of the key and the door should open—"

"Hush!" I cried, starting forward in horror of the thought he had suggested. "It is opening. I see a thread of light. What does it mean, Jupp? The child? No; there is more than a child's strength in that push. Hist!" Here I drew him flat against the wall. The door above had swung back and some one was stamping on the threshold over our heads in what appeared to be an outburst of ungovernable fury.

That it was the doctor I could not doubt. But why this anger; why this mad gasping after breath and the half-growl, half-cry, with which he faced the night and the quiet of a street which to his glance, passing as it did over our heads, must have appeared altogether deserted? We were consulting each other's faces for some explanation of this unlooked-for outbreak, when the door above us suddenly slammed to and we heard a renewal of that fumbling with lock and key which had first drawn our attention. But the hand was not sure or the hall was dark, for the key did not turn in the lock. Suddenly awake to my opportunity, I wheeled Jupp about and, making use of his knee and back, climbed up till I was enabled to reach the knob and turn it just as the man within had stepped back, probably to procure more light.

The result was that the door swung open and I stumbled in, falling almost face downward on the marble floor faintly checkered off to my sight in the dim light of a lamp set far back in a bare and dismal hall. I was on my feet again in an instant and it was in this manner, and with all the disadvantages of a hatless head and a disordered countenance, that I encountered again my old employer after five years of absence.

He did not recognize me. I saw it by the look of alarm which crossed his features and the involuntary opening of his lips in what would certainly have been a loud cry if I had not smiled and cried out with false gaiety:

"Excuse me, doctor, I never came in by that door before. Pardon my awkwardness. The step is somewhat high from the street."

My smile is my own, they say; at all events it served to enlighten him.

"Bob Trevitt," he exclaimed, but with a growl of displeasure I could hardly condemn under the circumstances.

I hastened to push my advantage, for he was looking very threateningly toward the door which was swaying gently and in an inviting way to a man who if old, had more power in his arms than I had in my whole body.

"Mr. Trevitt," I corrected; "and on a very important errand. I am here on behalf of Mrs. Ocumpaugh, whose child you have at this moment under your roof."

VI-DOCTOR POOL

It was a direct attack and for a minute I doubted if I had not made a mistake in making it so suddenly and without gloves. His face purpled, the veins on his forehead started out, his great form shook with an ire that in such domineering natures as his can only find relief in a blow. But the right hand did not rise nor the heavy fist fall. With admirable self-restraint he faced me for a moment, without attempting either protest or denial. Then his blazing eyes cooled down, and with a sudden gesture which at once relaxed his extreme tension of nerve and muscle, he pointed toward the end of the hall and remarked with studied politeness:

"My office is below, as you know. Will you oblige me by following me there?"

I feared him, for I saw that studiously as he sought to hide his impressions, he too regarded the moment as one of critical significance. But I assumed an air of perfect confidence, merely observing as I left the neighborhood of the front door and the proximity of Jupp:

"I have friends on the outside who are waiting for me; so you must not keep me too long."

He was bending to take up the lamp from a small table near the basement stair as I threw out these words in apparent carelessness, and the flash which shot from under his shaggy brows was thus necessarily heightened by the glare in which he stood. Yet with all allowances made I marked him down in my own mind as dangerous, and was correspondingly surprised when he turned on the top step of the narrow staircase I remembered so vividly from the experience I have before named, and in the mildest of accents remarked:

"These stairs are a trifle treacherous. Be careful to grasp the hand-rail as you come down."

Was the game deeper than I thought? In all my remembrance of him I had never before seen him look benevolent, and it alarmed me, coming as it did after the accusation I had made. I felt tempted to make a stand and demand that the interview be held then and there. For I knew his subterranean office very well, and how difficult it would be to raise a cry there which could be heard by any one outside. Still, with a muttered, "Thank you," I proceeded to follow him down, only stopping once in the descent to listen for some sound by which I could determine in which room of the many I knew to be on this floor the little one lay, on whose behalf I was incurring a possible bullet from the pistol I once saw lurking amongst bottles and corks in one of the innumerable drawers of the doctor's table. But all was still around and overhead; too still for my peace of mind, in which dreadful visions began to rise of a drugged or dying child, panting out its innocent breath in darkness and solitude. Yet no. With those thousands to be had for the asking, any man would be a fool to injure or even seriously to frighten a child upon whose good condition they depended; much less a miser whose whole heart was fixed on money.

The clock struck as I put foot on the landing; so much can happen in twenty minutes when events crowd and the passions of men reach their boiling-point! I expected to see the old man try that door, even to double bolt it as in the years gone by. But he merely threw a look that way and proceeded on down the three or four steps which led into the species of basement where he had chosen to fix his office. In another moment that dim and dismal room broke upon my view under the vague light of the small and poorly-trimmed lamp he carried. I saw again its musty walls covered with books, where there were shelves laden with bottles and a loose array of miscellaneous objects I had often handled but out of which I never could make any meaning. I recognized it all and detected but few changes. But these were startling ones. The old lounge standing under the two barred windows which I had often likened in my own mind to those of a jail, had been recovered; and lying on the table, which I had always regarded with a mixture of awe and apprehension, I perceived something which I had never seen there before: a Bible, with its edges worn and its leaves rumpled as if often and eagerly handled.

I was so struck by this last discovery that I stopped, staring, in the doorway, looking from the sacred volume to his worn but vigorous figure drawn up in the middle of the room, with the lamp still in his hand and his small but brilliant eyes fixed upon mine with a certain ironical glitter in them, which gave me my first distrust of the part I had come there to play.

"We will waste no words," said he, setting down the lamp, and seizing with his disengaged hand the long locks of his flowing beard. "In what respect are you a messenger from Mrs. Ocumpaugh, and what makes you think I have her child in this house?"

I found it easier to answer the last question first.

"I know the child is here," I replied, "because my partner saw you bring her in. I have gone into the detective business since leaving you."

"Ah!"

There was an astonishing edge to his smile and I felt that I should have to make the most of that old discovery of mine, if I were to hold my own with this man.

"And may I ask," he coldly continued, "how you have succeeded in connecting me with this young child's disappearance?"

"It's straight as a string," I retorted. "You threatened the child to its face in the hearing of its nurse some two weeks ago, on a certain bridge where you stopped them. You even set the day when the little Gwendolen should pass from luxury to poverty." Here I cast an involuntary glance about the room where the only sign of comfort was the newly upholstered lounge. "That day was the sixteenth, and we all know what happened on that date. If this is not plain enough—" I had seen his lip curl—"allow me to add, by way of explanation, that you have seen fit to threaten Mrs. Ocumpaugh herself with this date, for I know well the hand which wroteAugust 16on the bungalow floor and in various other places about Homewood where her eye was likely to fall." And I let my own fall on a sort of manuscript lying open not far from the Bible, which still looked so out of place to me on this pagan-hearted old miser's table. "Such chirography as yours is not to be mistaken," I completed, with a short gesture toward the disordered sheets he had left spread out to every eye.

"I see. A detective without doubt. Did you play the detective here?"

The last question leaped like a shot from his lips.

"You have not denied the threats to which I have just called your attention," was my cautious reply.

"What need of that?" he retorted. "Are you not a—detective?"

There was sarcasm, as well as taunt in the way he uttered that last word. I was conscious of being at a loss, but put a bold front on the matter and proceeded as if conscious of no secret misgiving.

"Can you deny as well that you have been gone two days from this place? That during this time a doctor's buggy, drawn by a horse I should know by description, having harnessed him three times a day for two years, was seen by more than one observer in the wake of a mysterious wagon from the interior of which a child's crying could be heard? The wagon did not drive up to this house to-night, but the buggy did, and from it you carried a child which you brought with you into this house."

With a sudden down-bringing of his old but powerful hand on the top of the table before him, he seemed about to utter an oath or some angry invective.

But again he controlled himself, and eying me without any show of shame or even of desire to contradict any of my assertions, he quietly declared:

"You are after that reward, I observe. Well, you won't get it. Like many others of your class you can follow a trail, but the insight to start right and to end in triumphant success is given only to a genius, and you are not a genius."

With a blush I could not control, I advanced upon him, crying:

"You have forestalled me. You have telegraphed or telephoned to Mr. Atwater—"

"I have not left my house since I came in here three hours ago."

"Then—" I began.

But he hushed me with a look.

"It is not a matter of money," he declared almost with dignity. "Those who think to reap dollars from the distress which has come upon the Ocumpaugh family will eat ashes for their pains. Money will be spent, but none of it earned, unless you, or such as you, are hired at so much an hour to—follow trails."

Greatly astounded not only by the attitude he took, but by the calm and almost indifferent way in which he mentioned what I had every reason to believe to be the one burning object of his existence, I surveyed him with undisguised astonishment till another thought, growing out of the silence of the many-roomed house above us, gripped me with secret dread; and I exclaimed aloud and without any attempt at subterfuge:

"She is dead, then! the child is dead!"

"I do not know," was his reply.

The four words were uttered with undeniable gloom.

"You do not know?" I echoed, conscious that my jaw had fallen, and that I was staring at him with fright in my eyes.

"No. I wish I did. I would give half of my small savings to know where that innocent baby is to-night. Sit down!" he vehemently commanded. "You do not understand me, I see. You confound the old Doctor Pool with the new."

"I confound nothing," I violently retorted in strong revulsion against what I had now come to look upon as the attempt of a subtle actor to turn aside my suspicions and brave out a dangerous situation by a ridiculous subterfuge. "I understand the miser whom I have beheld gloating over his hoard in the room above, and I understand the doctor who for money could lend himself to a fraud, the secret results of which are agitating the whole country at this moment."

"So!" The word came with difficulty. "So youdidplay the detective, even as a boy. Pity I had not recognized your talents at the time. But no—" he contradicted himself with great rapidity; "I was not a redeemed soul then; I might have done you harm. I might have had more if not worse sins to atone for than I have now." And with scant appearance of having noted the doubtful manner in which I had received this astonishing outburst, he proceeded to cry aloud and with a commanding gesture: "Quit this. You have undertaken more than you can handle. You, a messenger from Mrs. Ocumpaugh? Never. You are but the messenger of your own cupidity; and cupidity leads by the straightest of roads directly down to hell."

"This you proved six long years ago. Lead me to the child I believe to be in this house or I will proclaim aloud the pact you entered into then—a pact to which I was an involuntary witness whose word, however, will not go for less on that account. Behind the curtain still hanging over that old closet I stood while—"

His hand had seized my arm with a grip few could have proceeded under.

"Do you mean—"

The rest was whispered in my ear.

"DO YOU MEAN"—THE REST WAS WHISPERED IN MY EAR.

I nodded and felt that he was mine now. But the laugh which the next minute broke from his lips dashed my assurance.

"Oh, the ways of the world!" he cried. Then in a different tone and not without reverence: "Oh, the ways of God!"

I made no reply. For every reason I felt that the next word must come from him.

It was an unexpected one.

"That was Doctor Pool unregenerate and more heedful of the things of this world than of those of the world to come. You have to deal with quite a different man now. It is of that very sin I am now repenting in sackcloth and ashes. I live but to expiate it. Something has been done toward accomplishing this, but not enough. I have been played upon, used. This I will avenge. New sin is a poor apology for an old one."

I scarcely heeded him. I was again straining my ears to catch a smothered sob or a frightened moan.

"What are you listening for?" he asked.

"For the sound of little Gwendolen's voice. It is worth fifty thousand dollars, you remember. Why shouldn't I listen for it? Besides, I have a real and uncontrollable sympathy for the child. I am determined to restore her to her home. Your blasphemous babble of a changed heart does not affect me. You are after a larger haul than the sum offered by Mr. Ocumpaugh. You want some of Mrs. Ocumpaugh's fortune. I have suspected it from the first."

"I want? Little you know what I want"—then quickly, convincingly: "You are strangely deceived. Little Miss Ocumpaugh is not here."

"What is that I hear, then?" was the quick retort with which I hailed the sigh, unmistakably from infantile lips, which now rose from some place very much nearer us than the hollow regions overhead toward which my ears had been so long turned.

"That!" He flashed with uncontrollable passion, and if I am not mistaken clenched his hands so violently as to bury his nails in his flesh. "Would you like to see what that is? Come!"—and taking up the lamp, he moved, much to my surprise as well as to my intense interest, toward the door of the small cupboard where I had myself slept when in his service.

That he still meditated some deviltry which would call for my full presence of mind to combat successfully, I did not in the least doubt. Yet the agitation under which I crossed the floor was more the result of an immediate anticipation of seeing—and in this place of all others in the world—the child about whom my thoughts had clung so persistently for forty-two hours, than of any results to myself in the way of injury or misfortune. Though the room was small and my passage across it necessarily short, I had time to remember Mrs. Ocumpaugh's pitiful countenance as I saw it gazing in agony of expectation from her window overlooking the river, and to catch again the sounds, less true and yet strangely thrilling, of Mrs. Carew's voice as she said: "A tragedy at my doors and I occupied with my own affairs!" Nor was this all. A recollection of Miss Graham's sorrow came up before my eyes also, and, truest of all, most penetrating to me of all the loves which seemed to encompass this rare and winsome infant, the infinite tenderness with which I once saw Mr. Ocumpaugh lift her to his breast, during one of my interviews with him at Homewood.

All this before the door had swung open. Afterward, I saw nothing and thought of nothing but the small figure lying in the spot where I had once pillowed my own head, and with no more luxuries or even comforts about her than had been my lot under this broad but by no means hospitable roof.

A bare wall, a narrow cot, a table with a bottle and glass on it and the child in the bed—that was all. But God knows, it was enough to me at that breathless moment; and advancing eagerly, I was about to stoop over the little head sunk deep in its pillow, when the old man stepped between and with a short laugh remarked:

"There's no such hurry. I have something to say first, in explanation of the anger you have seen me display; an anger which is unseemly in a man professing to have conquered the sins and passions of lost humanity. I did follow this child. You were right in saying that it was my horse and buggy which were seen in the wake of the wagon which came from the region of Homewood and lost itself in the crossroads running between the North River and the Sound. For two days and a night I followed it, through more difficulties than I could relate in an hour, stopping in lonely woods, or at wretched taverns, watching, waiting for the transfer of the child, whose destination I was bound to know even if it cost me a week of miserable travel without comfortable food or decent lodging. I could hear the child cry out from time to time—an assurance that I was not following a will-o'-the-wisp—but not till to-day, not till very late to-day, did any words pass between me and the man and woman who drove the wagon. At Fordham, just as I suspected them of making final efforts to escape me, they came to a halt and I saw the man get out.

"I immediately got out too. As we faced each other, I demanded what the matter was. He appeared reckless. 'Are you a doctor?' he asked. I assured him that I was. At which he blurted out: 'I don't know why you've been following us so long, and I don't care. I've got a job for you. A child in our wagon is ill.'"

With a start I attempted to look over the old man's shoulder toward the bed. But the deep, if irregular, breathing of the child reassured me, and I turned to hear the doctor out.

"This gave me my chance. 'Let me see her,' I cried. The man's eye lowered. I did not like his face at all. 'If it's anything serious,' he growled, 'I shall cut. It isn't my flesh and blood nor yet my old woman's there. You'll have to find some place for the brat besides my wagon if it's anything that won't get cured without nu'ssin'. So come along and have a look.' I followed him, perfectly determined to take the child under my own care, sick or well. 'Where were you going to take her?' I asked. I didn't ask who she was; why should I? 'I don't know as I am obliged to tell,' was his surly reply. 'Where we are going oursel's,' he reluctantly added. 'But not to nu'ss. I've no time for nu'ssin' brats, nor my wife neither. We have a journey to make. Sarah!'—this to his wife, for by this time we were beside the wagon, 'lift up the flap and hold the youngster's hand out. Here's a doctor who will tell us if it's fever or not.' A puny hand and wrist were thrust out. I felt the pulse and then held out my arms. 'Give me the child,' I commanded. 'She's sick enough for a hospital.' A grunt from the woman within, an oath from the man, and a bundle was presently put in my arms, from which a little moan escaped as I strode with it toward my buggy. 'I do not ask your name,' I called back to the man who reluctantly followed me. 'Mine is Doctor Pool and I live in Yonkers.' He muttered something about not peachin' on a poor man who was really doin' an unfortunate a kindness, and then slunk hurriedly back and was gone, wagon, wife and all, by the time I had whipped up my tired old nag and turned about toward Yonkers. But I had the child safe and sound in my arms, and my fears of its fate were relieved. It was not well, but I anticipated nothing serious. When it moaned I pressed it a little closer to my breast and that was all. In three-quarters of an hour we were in Yonkers. In fifteen minutes I had it on this bed, and had begun to unroll the shawl in which it was closely wrapped. Did you ever see the child about whom there has been all this coil?"

"Yes, about three years ago."

"Three years! I have seen her within a fortnight; yet I could carry that young one in my arms for a whole hour without the least suspicion that I was making a fool of myself."

Quickly slipping aside, he allowed me to approach the bed and take my first look at the sleeping child's face. It was a sweet one but I did not need the hint he had given me to find the features strange, and lacking every characteristic of those of Gwendolen Ocumpaugh. Yet as the cutting off of the hair will often change the whole aspect of the face—and this child's hair was short—I was stooping in great excitement to notice more particularly the contour of cheek and chin which had given individuality to the little heiress, when the doctor touched me on the arm and drew my attention to a pair of little trousers and a shirt which were hanging on the door behind me.

"Those are the clothes I came upon under that great shawl. The child I have been following and whom I have brought into my house under the impression it was Gwendolen Ocumpaugh is not even a girl."

VII-"FIND THE CHILD!"

I could well understand the wrath to which this man had given way, by the feeling which now took hold of my own breast.

"A boy!" I exclaimed.

"A boy."

Still incredulous, I leaned over the child and lifted into the full light of the lamp one of the little hands I saw lying outside of the coverlet. There was no mistaking it for a girl's hand, let alone a little lady's.

"So we are both fools!" I vociferated in my unbounded indignation, careful however to lay the small hand gently back on the panting breast. And turning away both from the doctor and his small patient, I strolled back into the office.

The bubble whose gay colors I had followed with such avidity had burst in my face with a vengeance.

But once from under the influence of the doctor's sarcastic eye, my better nature reasserted itself. Wheeling about, I threw this question back:

"If that is a boy and a stranger, where is Gwendolen Ocumpaugh?"

A moan from the bed and a hurried movement on the part of the doctor, who took this opportunity to give the child another dose of medicine, were my sole response. Waiting till the doctor had finished his task and drawn back from the bedside, I repeated the question and with increased emphasis:

"Where, then, is Gwendolen Ocumpaugh?"

Still the doctor did not answer, though he turned my way and even stepped forward; his long visage, cadaverous from fatigue and the shock of his disappointment, growing more and more somber as he advanced.

When he came to a stand by the table, I asked again:

"Where is the child idolized by Mr. Ocumpaugh and mourned to such a degree by his almost maddened wife that they say she will die if the little girl is not found?"

The threat in my tones brought a response at last—a response which astonished me.

"Have I not said that I do not know? Do you not believe me? Do you think me as blind to-day to truth and honor as I was six years ago? Have you no idea of repentance and regeneration from sin? You are a detective. Find me that child. You shall have money — hundreds — thousands — if you can bring me proofs of her being yet alive. If the Hudson has swallowed her —" here his figure rose, dilated and took on a majesty which impressed itself upon me through all my doubts — "I will have vengeance on whoever has thus dared the laws of God and man as I would on the foulest murderer in the foulest slums of that city which breeds wickedness in high places as in low. I lock hands no longer with Belial. Find me the child, or make me at least to know the truth!"

There was no doubting the passion which drove these words hot from his lips. I recognized at last the fanatic whom Miss Graham had so graphically described in relating her extraordinary adventure on the bridge; and met him with this one question, which was certainly a vital one:

"Who dropped a shoe from the little one's closet, into the water under the dock? Did you?"

"No." His reply came quick and sharp.

"But," I insisted, "you have had something to do with this child's disappearance."

He did not answer. A sullen look was displacing the fire of resolve in the eyes I saw sinking slowly before mine.

"I will not acknowledge it," he muttered; adding, however, in what was little short of a growl: "Not yet, not till it becomes my duty to avenge innocent blood."

"You foretold the date."

"Drop it."

"You were in league with the abductor," I persisted. "I declare to your face, in spite of all the vaunted scruples with which you seek to blind me to your guilt, that you were in league with the abductor, knowing what money Mrs. Ocumpaugh would pay. Only he was too smart for you, and perhaps too unscrupulous. You would stop short of murder, now that you have got religion. But his conscience is not so nice and so you fear —"

"You do not know what I fear and I am not going to tell you. It is enough that I am conscious of my own uprightness and that I say, Find the child! You have incentive enough."

It was true and it was growing stronger every minute.

"Confine yourself to such clues as are apparent to every eye," he now admonished me with an eagerness that seemed real. "If they are pointed by some special knowledge you believe yourself to have gained, that is all the better — perhaps. I do not propose to say."

I saw that he had uttered his ultimatum.

"Very good," said I. "I have, nevertheless, one more question to ask which relates to those very clues. You can not refuse to answer it if you are really desirous of aiding me in my efforts. Where did you first come upon the wagon which you followed so many hours in the belief that it held Gwendolen Ocumpaugh?"

He mused a moment with downcast head, his nervous frame trembling with the force with which he threw his whole weight on the hand he held outspread on the table before him. Then he calmly replied:

"I will tell you that. At the gate of Mrs. Carew's grounds. You know them? They adjoin the Ocumpaughs' on the left."

My surprise made me lower my head but not so quickly that I did not catch the oblique glint of his eye as he mentioned the name which I was so little prepared to hear in this connection.

"I was in my buggy on the highroad," he continued. "There was a constant passing by of all kinds of vehicles on their way to and from the Ocumpaugh entertainment, but none that attracted my attention till I caught sight of the covered wagon I have endeavored to describe, being driven out of the adjoining grounds. Then I pricked up my ears, for a child was crying inside in the smothered way that tells of a hand laid heavily over the mouth. I thought I knew what child this was, but you have been a witness to my disappointment after forty-eight hours of travel behind that wretched wagon."

"It came out of Mrs. Carew's grounds?" I repeated, ignoring everything but the one important fact. "And during the time, you say, when Mrs. Ocumpaugh's guests were assembling? Did you see any other vehicle leave by the same gate at or before that time?"

"Yes, a carriage. It appeared to have no one in it. Indeed, I know that it was empty, for I peered into it as it rolled by me down the street. Of course I do not know what might have been under the seats."

"Nothing," was my sharp retort. "That was the carriage in which Mrs. Carew had come up from the train. Did it pass out before the wagon?"

"Yes, by some minutes."

"There is nothing, then, to be gained by that."

"There does not seem to be."

Was his accent in uttering this simple phrase peculiar? I looked up to make sure. But his face, which had been eloquent with one feeling or another during every minute of this long interview till the present instant, looked strangely impassive, and I did not know how to press the question hovering on my lips.

"You have given me a heavy task," I finally remarked, "and you offer very little assistance in the way of conjecture. Yet you must have formed some."

He toyed with his beard, combing it with his nervous, muscular fingers, and as I watched how he lingered over the tips, caressing them before he dropped them, I felt that he was toying with my perplexities in much the same fashion and with an equal satisfaction. Angry and out of all patience with him, I blurted out:

"I will do without your aid. I will solve this mystery and earn your money if not that of Mr. Ocumpaugh, with no assistance save that afforded by my own wits."

"I expect you will," he retorted; and for the first time since I burst in upon him like one dropping from the clouds through the unapproachable doorway on the upper floor, he lost that look of extreme tension which had nerved his aged figure into something of the aspect of youth. With it vanished his impressiveness. It was simply a tired old man I now followed upstairs to the side door. As I paused to give him a final nod and an assurance of intended good faith toward him, he made a kindly enough gesture in the direction of my old room below and said:

"Don't worry about the little fellow down there. He'll come out all right. I shan't visit on him the extravagance of my own folly. I am a Christian now." And with this encouraging remark he closed the door and I found myself alone in the dark alley.

My first sense of relief came from the coolness of the night air on my flushed forehead and cheeks. After the stifling atmosphere of this underground room, reeking with the fumes of the lamp and the heat of a struggle which his dogged confidence in himself had made so unequal, it was pleasurable just to sense the quiet and the cool of the night and feel myself released from the bondage of a presence from which I had frequently recoiled but had never thoroughly felt the force of till to-night; my next, from the touch and voice of my partner who at that moment rose from before the basement windows where he had evidently been lying for a long time outstretched.

"What have you two been doing down there?" was his very natural complaint. "I tried to listen, I tried to see; but beyond a few scattered words when your voices rose to an excited pitch, I have learned nothing but that you were in no danger save from the overthrow of your scheme. That has failed, has it not? You would have interrupted me long ago if you had found the child."

"Yes," I acknowledged; drawing him down the alley, "I have failed for to-night, but I start afresh to-morrow. Though how I can rest idle for nine hours, not knowing under what roof, if under any, that doomed innocent may be lying, I do not know."

"You must rest; you are staggering with fatigue now."

"Not a bit of it, only with uncertainty. I don't see my way. Let us go down street and see if any news has come over the wires since I left Homewood."

"But first, what a spooky old house that is! And what did the old gentleman have to say of your tumbling in on him from space without a 'By your leave' or even an 'Excuse me'? Tell me about it."

I told him enough to allay his curiosity. That was all I thought necessary,— and he seemed satisfied. Jupp is a good fellow, quite willing to confine himself to his particular end of the business which does not include the thinking end. Why should it?

There was no news—this we soon learned—only some hints of a contemplated move on the part of the police in a district where some low characters had been seen dragging along a resisting child of an unexpectedly refined appearance. As no one could describe this child and as I had refused from the first to look upon this case as one of ordinary abduction, I laid little stress on the report, destined though it was to appear under startling head-lines on the morrow, and startled my more credulous partner quite out of his usual equanimity, by ordering him on our arrival at the station to buy me a ticket for − −, as I was going back to Homewood.

"To Homewood, so late!"

"Exactly. It will not be late there—or if it is, anxious hearts make light sleepers."

His shoulders rose a trifle, but he bought the ticket.

VIII-"PHILO! PHILO! PHILO!"

Never have I felt a weirder sensation than when I stepped from the cars on to the solitary platform from which a few hours before I had seen the little nursery-governess depart for New York. The train, soon to disappear in the darkness of the long perspective, was all that gave life and light to the scene, and when it was gone, nothing remained to relieve the gloom or to break the universal stillness save the quiet lap of the water and the moaning of the wind through the trees which climbed the heights to Homewood.

I had determined to enter if possible by way of the private path, though I expected to find it guarded against just such intrusion. In approaching it I was given a full view of the river and thus was in a position to note that the dock and adjoining banks were no longer bright with lanterns in the hands of eager men bending with fixed eyes over the flowing waters. The search which had kept so many busy at this spot for well on to two days had been abandoned; and the darkness seemed doubly dark and the silence doubly oppressive in contrast.

Yet hope spoke in the abandonment; and with renewed spirit and a more than lively courage, I turned toward the little gate through which I had passed twice before that day. As I expected, a silent figure rose up from the shadows to prevent me; but it fell back at the mention of my name and business, thus proving the man to be in the confidence of Mrs. Ocumpaugh or, at the least, in that of Miss Porter.

"I am come for a social chat with the coachman," I explained. "Lights burn late in such extensive stables. Don't worry about me. The people at the house are in sympathy with my investigation."

Thus we stretch the truth at great crises.

"I know you," was the answer. "But keep away from the house. Our orders are imperative to allow no one to approach it again to-night, except with the child in hand or with such news as would gain instant admission."

"Trust me," said I, as I went up the steps.

It was so dark between the hedge-rows that my ascent became mere groping. I had a lantern in my pocket which I had taken from Jupp, but I did not choose to make use of it. I preferred to go on and up, trusting to my instinct to tell me when I had reached a fresh flight of steps.

A gleam of light from Mrs. Carew's upper windows was the first intimation I received that I was at the top of the bank, and in another moment I was opposite the gap in the hedge opening upon her grounds.

For no particular reason that I know of, I here paused and took a long survey of what was, after all, nothing but a cluster of shadows broken here and there by squares of subdued light. I felt a vague desire to enter — to see and talk again with the charming woman whose personality had made such an impression upon me, if only to understand the peculiar feelings which those indistinguishable walls awakened, and why such a sense of anticipation should disturb my admiration of this woman and the delight which I had experienced in every accent of her trained and exquisite voice.

I was standing very still and in almost total darkness. The shock, therefore, was great when, in finally making up my mind to move, I became conscious of a presence near me, totally indiscernible and as silent as myself.

Whose?

No watchman, or he would have spoken at the rustle I made stumbling back against the hedge-row. Some marauder, then, or a detective, like myself? I would not waste time in speculating; better to decide the question at once, for the situation was eery, the person, whoever he was, stood so near and so still, and so directly in the way of my advance.

Drawing the lantern from my pocket, I pushed open the slide and flashed the light on the immovable figure before me. The face I beheld staring into mine was one quite unknown to me, but as I took in its expression, my arm gradually fell, and with it the light from the man's features, till face and form were lost again in the darkness, leaving in my disturbed mind naught but an impression; but such an impression!

The countenance thus flashed upon my vision must have been a haunting one at any time, but seen as I saw it, at a moment of extreme self-abandonment, the effect was startling. Yet I had sufficient control over myself to utter a word or two of apology, which was not answered, if it was even heard.

A more exact description may be advisable. The person whom I thus encountered hesitating before Mrs. Carew's house was a man of meager build, sloping shoulders and handsome but painfully pinched features. That he was a gentleman of culture and the nicest refinement was evident at first glance; that this culture and refinement were at this moment under the dominion of some fierce thought or resolve was equally apparent, giving to his look an absorption which the shock attending the glare I had thus suddenly thrown on his face could not immediately dispel.

Dazed by an encounter for which he seemed even less prepared than myself, he stood with his heart in his face, if I may so speak, and only gradually came to himself as the sense of my proximity forced itself in upon his suffering and engrossed mind. When I saw that he had quite emerged from his dream, I dropped the light. But I did not forget his look; I did not forget the man, though I hastened to leave him, in my desire to fulfill the purpose for which I had entered these grounds at so late an hour.

My plan was, as I have said, to visit the Ocumpaugh stables and have a chat with the coachman. I had no doubt of my welcome and not much doubt of myself. Yet as I left the vicinity of Mrs. Carew's cottage and came upon the great house of the Ocumpaughs looming in the moonlight above its marble terraces, I felt impressed as never before both by the beauty and magnificence of the noble pile, and shrank with something like shame from the presumption which had led me to pit my wits against a mystery having its birth in so much grandeur and material power. The prestige of great wealth as embodied in this superb structure well-nigh awed me from my task and I was passing the twin pergolas and flower-bordered walks with hesitating foot, when I heard through one of the open windows a cry which made me forget everything but our common heritage of sorrow and the equal hold it has on high and low.

"Philo!" the voice rang out in a misery to wring the heart of the most callous. "Philo! Philo!"

Mr. Ocumpaugh's name called aloud by his suffering wife. Was she in delirium? It would seem so; but why Philo! always Philo! and not once Gwendolen?

With hushed steps, ears ringing and heart palpitating with new and indefinable sensations, I turned into the road to the stables.

There were men about and I caught one glimpse of a maid's pretty head looking from one of the rear windows, but no one stopped me, and I reached the stable just as a man came sauntering out to take his final look at the weather.

It was the fellow I sought, Thomas the coachman.

I had not miscalculated the nature of my man. In ten minutes we were seated together on an open balcony, smoking and beguiling the time with a little harmless gossip. After a free and easy discussion of the great event, mingled with the naturally-to-be-expected criticism of the police, we proceeded under my guidance to those particulars for which I had risked losing this very valuable hour.

He mentioned Mrs. Ocumpaugh; I mentioned Mrs. Carew.

"A beautiful woman," I remarked.

I thought he looked astonished. "Shebeautiful?" was his doubtful rejoinder. "What do you think of Mrs. Ocumpaugh?"

"She is handsome, too, but in a different way."

"I should think so. I've driven rich and I've driven poor. I've even sat on the box in front of an English duchess, but never have I seen such features as Mrs. Ocumpaugh's. That's why I consent to drive an American millionaire's wife when I might be driving the English nobility."

"A statue!" said I; "cold!"

"True enough, but one you never tire of looking at. Besides, she can light up wonderfully. I've seen her when she was all a-quiver, and lovely as the loveliest. And when do you think that was?"

"When she had her child in her arms."

I spoke in lowered tones as befitted the suggestion and the circumstances.

"No," he drawled, between thoughtful puffs of smoke; "when Mr. Ocumpaugh sat on the seat beside her. This, when I was driving the victoria. I often used to make excuse for turning my head about so as to catch a glimpse of her smile at some fine view and the way she looked up at him to see if he was enjoying it as much as she. I like women who love their husbands."

"And he?"

"Oh, she has nothing to complain of in him. He worships the ground she walks on; and he more than worshiped the child."

Herehisvoice fell.

I brought the conversation back as quickly as I could to Mrs. Carew.

"You like pale women," said I. "Now I like a woman who looks plain one minute, and perfectly charming the next."

"That's what people say of Mrs. Carew. I know of lots who admire that kind. The little girl for one."

"Gwendolen? Was she attracted to Mrs. Carew?"

"Attracted? I've seen her go to her from her mother's lap like a bird to its nest. Many a time have I driven the carriage with Mrs. Ocumpaugh sitting up straight inside, and her child curled up in this other woman's arms with not a look or word for her mother."

"How did Mrs. Ocumpaugh seem to like that?" I asked between puffs of my cigar.

"Oh, she's one of the cold ones, you know! At least you say so; but I feel sure that for the last three years — that is, ever since this woman came into the neighborhood — her heart has been slowly breaking. This last blow will kill her."

I thought of the moaning cry of "Philo! Philo!" which at intervals I still seemed to hear issue from that upper window in the great house, and felt that there might be truth in his fears.

But it was of Mrs. Carew I had come to talk and not of Mrs. Ocumpaugh.

"Children's fancies are unaccountable," I sententiously remarked; "but perhaps there is some excuse for this one. Mrs. Carew has what you call magnetism — a personality which I should imagine would be very appealing to a child. I never saw such expression in a human face. Whatever her mood, she impresses each passing feeling upon you as the one reality of her life. I can not understand such changes, but they are very fascinating."

"Oh, they are easy enough to understand in her case. She was an actress once. I myself have seen her on the stage — in London. I used to admire her there."

"An actress!" I repeated, somewhat taken aback.

"Yes, I forget what name she played under. But she's a very great lady now; in with all the swells and rich enough to own a yacht if she wanted to."

"But a widow."

"Oh, yes, a widow."

I let a moment of silence pass, then nonchalantly remarked:

"Why is she going to Europe?"

But this was too much for my simple-hearted friend. He neither knew nor had any conjecture ready. But I saw that he did not deplore her resolve. His reason for this presently appeared.

"If the little one is found, the mother will want all her caresses. Let Mrs. Carew hug the boy that God in his mercy has thrown into her arms and leave other children to their mothers."

I rose to leave, when I bethought me and stopped to ask another question.

"Who is the gentleman I have seen about here — a man with a handsome face, but very pale and thin in his appearance, so much so that it is quite noticeable?"

"Do you mean Mr. Rathbone?"

"I do not know his name. A light complexioned man, who looks as if greatly afflicted by some disease or secret depression."

"Oh, that is Mr. Rathbone, sure. He is sickly-looking enough and not without his trouble, too. They say—but it's all gossip, of course—that he has set his heart on the widow."

"Mrs. Carew?"

"Of course, who else?"

"And she?"

"Why, she would be a fool to care for him, unless—"

"Unless what?"

Thomas laughed—a little uneasily, I could not help thinking.

"I'm afraid we're talking scandal," said he. "You know the relationship?"

"What relationship?"

"Why, his relationship to the family. He is Gwendolen's cousin and I have heard it said that he's named after her in Madam Ocumpaugh's will."

"O, I see! The next heir, eh?"

"Yes, to the Rathbone property."

"So that if she is not found—"

"Your sickly man, in that case, would be well worth the marrying."

"Is Mrs. Carew so fond of money as all that? I thought she was a woman of property."

"She is; but it takes money to make some men interesting. He isn't handsome enough, or independent enough to go entirely on his own merits. Besides, he has a troop of relatives hanging on to him—blood-suckers who more than eat up his salary."

"A business man, then?"

"Yes, in some New York house. He was always very fond of Gwendolen, and I am not surprised to hear that he is very much cut up by our trouble. I always thought well of Mr. Rathbone myself,"—which same ended the conversation so far as my interest in it was concerned.

IX-THE BUNGALOW

As soon as I could break away and leave him I did, and betook myself to Mrs. Carew's house. My resolve was taken. Late as it was, I would attempt an interview with her. The lights still burning above and below gave me the necessary courage. Yet I was conscious of some embarrassment in presenting my name to the astonished maid, who was in the act of extinguishing the hall-light when my vigorous ring prevented her. Seeing her doubtful look and the hesitation with which she held the door, I told her that I would wait outside on the porch till she had carried up my name to Mrs. Carew. This seemed to relieve her and in a moment I was standing again under the vines waiting for permission to enter the house. It came very soon, and I had to conquer a fresh embarrassment at the sight of Mrs. Carew's nimble and gracious figure descending the stairs in all eagerness to greet me.

"What is it?" she asked, running hastily forward so that we met in the center of the hall. "Good news? Nothing else could have brought you back again so soon—and at an hour so late."

There was a dangerous naïveté in the way she uttered the last three words which made me suspect the actress. Indeed I was quite conscious as I met her thrilling and expressive glance, that I should never feel again the same confidence in her sincerity. My judgment had been confounded and my insight rendered helpless by what I had heard of her art, and the fact that she had once been a capable player of "parts."

But I was man enough and detective enough not to betray my suspicion, now that I was brought face to face with her. It had always been latent in my breast, even in the very midst of my greatest admiration for her. Yet I had never acknowledged to myself of what I suspected her, nor did I now—not quite—not enough to give that point to my attack which would have insured me immediate victory or defeat. I was obliged to feel my way and so answered, with every appearance of friendly confidence:

"I fear then that I shall be obliged to ask your pardon. I have no good news; rather what might be called, if not bad, of a very perplexing character. The child has been traced"—here I purposely let my voice halt for an instant—"here."

"Here?" her eyes opened, her lips parted in a look of surprise so ingenuous that involuntarily I felt forced to add, by way of explanation:

"The child, I mean, who was carried screaming along the highway in a wagon and for whom the police—and others—have for two days been looking."

"Oh!" she ejaculated with a slight turn of her head aside as she motioned me toward a chair. "And is that child Gwendolen? Or don't you know?" She was all eagerness as she again faced me.

"That will be known to-morrow," I rejoined, resisting the beautiful brightness of her face with an effort that must have left its mark on my own features; for she smiled with unconscious triumph as she held my eyes for a minute in hers saying softly, "O how you excite me! Tell me more. Where was the wagon found? Who is with it? And how much of all this have you told Mrs. Ocumpaugh?"

With the last question she had risen, involuntarily, it seemed, and as though she would rush to her friend if I did not at once reassure her of that friend's knowledge of a fact which seemed to throw a gleam of hope upon a situation hitherto entirely unrelieved.

"Mrs. Ocumpaugh has been told nothing," I hastily returned, answering the last and most important question first. "Nor must she be; at least not till certainty replaces doubt. She is in a critical state, I am told. To rouse her hopes to-night only to dash them again to-morrow would be cruel policy."

With her eyes still on my face, Mrs. Carew slowly reseated herself. "Then there are doubts," she faltered; "doubts of its being Gwendolen?"

"There is always doubt," I replied, and openly paused in manifest non-committal.

"Oh!" she somewhat wildly exclaimed, covering her face with her hands—beautiful hands covered with jewels—"what suspense! what bitter and cruel suspense! I feel it almost as much as if it were my Harry!" was the final cry with which she dropped them again. And she did feel it. Her features had blanched and her form was shaking. "But you have not answered my questions as to where this wagon is at present and under whose care? Can't you see how anxious I must be about that—if it should prove to be Gwendolen?"

"Mrs. Carew, if I could tell you that, I could tell you more; we shall both have to wait till to-morrow. Meanwhile, I have a favor to ask. Have you by any chance the means of entrance to the bungalow? I have a great and inappeasable desire to see for myself if all the nooks and corners of that place have given up their secrets. It's an egotistical desire, no doubt—and may strike you as folly of the rankest—but we detectives have learned to trust nobody in our investigations, and I shall never be satisfied till I have looked this whole spot over inch by inch for the clue which may yet remain there. If there is a clue I must find it."

"Clue?" She was looking at me a little breathlessly. "Clue to what? Then she wasn't in the wagon; you are still seeking her—"

"Always seeking her," I put in.

"But surely not in the bungalow!" Mrs. Carew's expression was one of extreme surprise. "What can you find there?"

"I do not know. But I want to look. I can go to the house for a key, but it is late; and it seems unpardonable to disturb Mrs. Ocumpaugh. Yet I shall have to do this if you have not a key; for I shall not sleep till I have satisfied myself that nothing can be discovered on the immediate scene of Gwendolen's disappearance, to help forward the rescue we both are so intent upon."

"You are right," was the hesitating reply I received. "I have a key; I will fetch it and if you do not mind, I will accompany you to the bungalow."

"Nothing would give me greater pleasure," I replied with my best bow; white lies come easy in our trade.

"I will not keep you a minute," she said, rising and going into the hall. But in an instant she was back. "A word to my maid and a covering for my head," she explained, "and I will be with you." Her manner pointed unmistakably to the door.

I had no alternative but to step out on the porch to await her. But she was true to her word and in a moment she had joined me, with the key in her hand.

"Oh, what adventures!" was her breathless cry. "Shall I ever forget this dreadful, this interminable week! But it is dark. Even the moon is clouded over. How shall we see? There are no lights in the bungalow."

"I have a lantern in my pocket. My only hope is that no stray gleam from it may pierce the shrubbery and bring the police upon us."

"Do you fear the police?" she chatted away, almost as a child might.

"No; but I want to do my work alone. There will be little glory or little money in it if they share any of my discoveries."

"Ah!" It was an irrepressible exclamation, or so it seemed: but I should not have noted it if I had not caught, or persuaded myself that I had caught, the oblique glint from her eye which accompanied it. But it was very dark just at this time and I could be sure of nothing but that she kept close to my side and seemed more than once on the point of addressing me in the short distance we traversed before reaching the bungalow. But nothing save inarticulate murmurs left her lips and soon we were too busy, in our endeavors to unlock the door, to think of conversation.

The key she had brought was rusty. Evidently she had not often made use of it. But after a few futile efforts I succeeded in making it work, and we stepped into the small building in a silence that was only less profound than the darkness in which we instantly found ourselves enveloped. Light was under my hand, however, and in another moment there opened before us the small square room whose every feature had taken on a ghostly and unfamiliar air from the strange hour and the unwonted circumstances. I saw how her impressionable nature was affected by the scene, and made haste to assume the offhand air I thought most likely to overcome her apprehension. But the effect of the blank walls before her, relieved, but in no reassuring way, by the long dark folds of the rugs hanging straight down over the mysterious partition, held its own against my well-meant efforts, and I was not surprised to hear her voice falter as she asked what I expected to find there.

I pointed to a chair and said:

"If you will sit down, I will show you, not what I expect to find, but how a detective goes about his work. Whatever our expectations, however small or however great, we pay full attention to details. Now the detail which has worried me in regard to this place is the existence of a certain space in this building unaccounted for by these four walls; in other words, the portion which lies behind these rugs," — and throwing aside the same, I let the flame from my lantern play over the walled-up space which I had before examined with little satisfaction. "This partition," I continued, "seems as firm as any of the walls, but I want to make sure that it hides nothing. If the child should be in some hole back of this partition, what a horror and what an outrage!"

"But it is impossible!" came almost in a shriek from the woman behind me. "The opening is completely walled up. I have never known of its being otherwise. It looked like that when I came here three years ago. There is no possible passage through that wall."

"Why was it ever closed up? Do you know?"

"Not exactly. The family are very reticent about it. Some fancy of Mr. Ocumpaugh's father, I believe. He was an odd man; they tell all manner of stories about him. If anything offended him, he rid himself of it immediately. He took a distaste to that end of the hut, as they used to call it in the old days before it was remodeled to suit the house, so he had it walled up. That is all we know about it."

"I wish I could see behind that wall," I muttered, dropping back the rug I had all this time held in my hand. "I feel some mystery here which I can not grasp." Then as I flashed my lantern about in every direction with no visible result, added with the effort which accompanies such disappointments: "There is nothing here, Mrs. Carew. Though it is the scene of the child's disappearance it gives me nothing."

X-TEMPTATION

The sharp rustle of her dress as she suddenly rose struck upon my ear.

"Then let us go," she cried, with just a slight quiver of eagerness in her wonderful voice. I comprehended its culture now. "The place is ghostly at this hour of the night. I believe that I am really afraid."

With a muttered reassurance, I allowed the full light of the lantern to fall directly on her face. Shewasafraid. There was no other explanation possible for her wild staring eyes and blue quivering lips. For the instant I hardly knew her; then her glance rose to mine and she smiled and it was with difficulty I refrained from acknowledging in words my appreciation of her wonderful flexibility of expression.

"You are astonished to see me so affected," she said. "It is not so strange as you think—it is superstition—the horror of what once happened here—the reason for that partition—I know the whole story, for all my attempts to deny it just now. The hour, too, is unfortunate—the darkness—your shifting, mysterious light. It was late like this—and dark—with just the moon to illumine the scene, when she—Mr. Trevitt, do you want to know the story of this place?—the old, much guessed-at, never-really-understood story which led first to its complete abandonment, then to the building of that dividing wall and finally to the restoration of this portion and of this alone? Do you?"

Her eagerness, in such startling contrast to the reticence she had shown on this very subject a few minutes before, affected me peculiarly. I wanted to hear the story—any one would who had listened to the gossip of this neighborhood for years, but—

She evidently did not mean to give me time to understand my own hesitation.

"I have the whole history—the touching, hardly-to-be-believed history—up at my house at this very moment. It was written by—no, I will let you guess."

The naïveté of her smile made me forget the force of its late expression.

"Mr. Ocumpaugh?" I ventured.

"Which Mr. Ocumpaugh? There have been so many." She began slowly, naturally, to move toward the door.

"I can not guess."

"Then I shall have to tell you. It was written by the one who—Come! I will tell you outside. I haven't any courage here."

"But I have."

"You haven't read the story."

"Never mind; tell me who the writer was."

"Mr. Ocumpaugh's father; he, by whose orders this partition was put up."

"Oh, you havehisstory—written—and by himself! You are fortunate, Mrs. Carew."

I had turned the lantern from her face, but not so far that I did not detect the deep flush which dyed her whole countenance at these words.

"I am," she emphatically returned, meeting my eyes with a steady look I was not sufficiently expert with women's ways, or at all events with this woman's ways, to understand. "Seldom has such a tale been written—seldom, let us thank God, has there been an equal occasion for it."

"You interest me," I said.

And she did. Little as this history might have to do with the finding of Gwendolen, I felt an almost imperative necessity of satisfying my curiosity in regard to it, though I knew she had deliberately roused this curiosity for a purpose which, if not comprehensible to me, was of marked importance to her and not altogether for the reason she had been pleased to give me. Possibly it was on account of this last mentioned conviction that I allowed myself to be so interested.

"It is late," she murmured with a final glance towards those dismal hangings which in my present mood I should not have been so greatly surprised to see stir under her look. "However, if you will pardon the hour and accept a seat in my small library, I will show you what only one other person has seen besides myself."

It was a temptation; for several reasons it was a temptation; yet—

"I want you to see why I am frightened of this place," she said, flashing her eyes upon me with an almost girlish appeal.

"I will go," said I; and following her quickly out, I locked the bungalow door, and ignoring the hand she extended toward me, dropped the key into my pocket.

I thought I heard a little gasp — the least, the smallest of sounds possible. But if so, the feeling which prompted it was not apparent in her manner or her voice as she led the way back to her house, and ushered me into a hall full of packing-boxes and the general litter accompanying an approaching departure.

"You will excuse the disorder," she cried as she piloted me through these various encumbrances to a small but exquisitely furnished room still glorying in its full complement of ornaments and pictures. "This trouble which has come to one I love has made it very hard for me to do anything. I feel helpless, at times, completely helpless."

The dejection she expressed was but momentary, however. In another instant she was pointing out a chair and begging me to make myself comfortable while she went for the letter (I think she called it a letter) which I had come there to read.

What was I to think of her? What was I to think of myself? And what would the story tell me to warrant the loss of what might have proved a most valuable hour? I had not answered these questions when she reëntered with a bundle in her hand of discolored — I should almost call them mouldered — sheets of much crumpled paper.

"These —" she began; then, seeing me look at them with something like suspicion, she paused until she caught my eye, when she added gravely, "these came to me from Mrs. Ocumpaugh. How she got them you will have to ask her. I should say, judging from appearances —" Here she took a seat opposite me at a small table near which I had been placed — "that they must have been found in some old chest or possibly in some hidden drawer of one of those curious antique desks of which more than one was discovered in the garrets of the old house when it was pulled down to give place to the new one."

"Is this letter, as you call it, so old?" I asked.

"It is dated thirty-five years ago."

"The garret must have been a damp one," I remarked.

She flashed me a look — I thought of it more than once afterward — and asked if she should do the reading or I.

"You," I rejoined, all afire with the prospect of listening to her remarkable voice in what I had every reason to believe would call forth its full expression. "Only let me look at those sheets first, and understand as perfectly as I may, just what it is you are going to read to me."

"It's an explanation written for his heirs by Mr. Ocumpaugh. The story itself," she went on, handing me over the papers she held, "begins abruptly.

From the way the sheet is torn across at the top, I judge that the narrative itself was preceded by some introductory words now lacking. When I have read it to you, I will tell you what I think those introductory words were."

I handed back the sheets. There seemed to be a spell in the air—possibly it arose from her manner, which was one to rouse expectation even in one whose imagination had not already been stirred by a visit at night and in more than commonly bewildering company to the place whose dark and hitherto unknown secret I was about to hear.

"I am ready," I said, feeling my strange position, but not anxious to change it just then for any other conceivable one.

She drew a deep breath; again fixed me with her strange, compelling eyes, and with the final remark:

"The present no longer exists, we are back in the seventies—" began this enthralling tale.

I did not move till the last line dropped from her lips.

XI-THE SECRET OF THE OLD PAVILION

I was as sane that night as I had ever been in my life. I am quite sure of this, though I had had a merry time enough earlier in the evening with my friends in the old pavilion (that time-honored retreat of my ancestors), whose desolation I had thought to dissipate with a little harmless revelry. Wine does not disturb my reason — the little wine I drank under that unwholesome roof — nor am I a man given to sudden excitements or untoward impulses.

Yet this thing happened to me.

It was after leaving the pavilion. My companions had all ridden away and I was standing on the lawn beyond my library windows, recalling my pleasure with them and gazing somewhat idly, I own, at that bare portion of the old wall where the tree fell a year ago (the place where the moon strikes with such a glitter when it rides high, as it did that night), when — believe it or not, it is all one to me — I became conscious of a sudden mental dread, inexplicable and alarming, which, seizing me after an hour of unmixed pleasure and gaiety, took such a firm grip upon my imagination that I fain would have turned my back upon the night and its influences, only my eyes would not leave that open space of wall where I now saw pass — not the shadow, but the veritable body of a large, black, hungry-looking dog, which, while I looked, turned into the open gateway connecting with the pavilion and disappeared.

With it went the oppression which held me spell-bound. The ice melted from my blood; I could move my limbs, and again control my thoughts and exercise my will.

Forcing a laugh, I whistled to that dog. The lights with which the banquet had been illuminated were out, and every servant had left the place; but the tables had not been entirely cleared, and I could well understand what had drawn this strange animal thither. I whistled then, and whistled peremptorily; but no dog answered my call. Angry, for the rules are strict at my stables in regard to wandering brutes, I strode toward the pavilion. Entering the great gap in the wall where a gate had once hung, I surveyed the dismal interior before me, with feelings I could not but consider odd in a strong man like myself. Though the wine was scarcely dry in the glass which an hour before

I had raised in this very spot amid cheers and laughter, I found it a difficult matter to reënter there now, in the dead of night, alone and without light.

For this building, harmless as it had always seemed, had been, in a way, cursed. For no reason that he ever gave, my father had doomed this ancient adjunct to our home to perpetual solitude and decay. By his will he had forbidden it to be destroyed—a wish respected by my guardians and afterward by myself—and though there was nothing to hinder its being cared for and in a manner used, the dismal influence which had pervaded the place ever since his death had, under the sensations I have mentioned, deepened into horror and an unspeakable repugnance.

Yet never having had any reason to believe myself a coward, I took boldly enough the few steps necessary to carry me inside its dismal precincts; and meeting with nothing but darkness and silence, began to whistle again for the dog I had certainly seen enter here.

But no dog appeared.

Hastening out, I took my way toward the stables. As I did so I glanced back, and again my eyes fell on that place in the wall gleaming white in the moonlight. Again I felt the chill, the horror! Again my eyes remained glued to this one spot; and again I beheld the passing of that dog, running with jaws extended and head held low—fearsome, uncanny, supernaturally horrible; a thing to flee from, if one could only flee instead of standing stock-still on the sward, gazing with eyes that seemed starting from their sockets till it had plunged through that gap in the wall and again disappeared.

The occult and the imaginary have never appealed to me, and the moment I felt myself a man again, I hurried on to the stables to call up my man Jared.

But half-way there I paused, struck by an odd remembrance. This father of mine, Philo Ocumpaugh, had died, or so his old servants had said, under peculiar circumstances. I had forgotten them till now—such stories make poor headway with me—but if I was not mistaken, the facts were these:

He had been ailing long, and his nurses had got used to the sight of his gaunt, white figure sitting propped up, but speechless, in the great bed opposite the stretch of blank wall in the corner bedroom, where a picture of his first wife, the wife of his youth, had once hung, but which, for some years now, had been removed to where there were fewer shadows and more sunlight. He had never been a talkative man, and in all the five years of my own memory of him, I had never heard him raise his voice except in command, or when the duties of hospitality required it. Now, with the shadow of death upon him, he was absolutely speechless, and his nurses were obliged to guess at his wishes by the movement of his hands or the direction of his eyes. Yet he was not morose, and sometimes was seen to struggle with the guards holding his tongue, as though he would fain have loosed himself from their inexorable control. Yet he never succeeded in doing so, and the nurses sat by and saw no difference in him, till suddenly the candle, posed on a table near by, flickered and went out, leaving only moonlight in the room. It was moonlight so brilliant that the place seemed brighter than before, though the beams were all concentrated on one spot, a blank space in the middle of the wall upon which those two dim orbs in the bed were fixed in an expectancy none there understood, for none knew that the summons had come, and that for him the angel of death was at that moment standing in the room.

Yet as moonlight is not the natural light for a sick man's bedside, one amongst them had risen for another candle, when something—I had never stopped to hear them say what—made him pause and look back, when he saw distinctly outlined upon the white wall-space I have mentioned, the figure—the unimaginable figure of a dog, large, fierce and hungry-looking, which dashed by and—was gone. Simultaneously a cry came from the bed, the first words for months—"Aline!"—the name of his girl-wife, dead and gone for years. All sprang; some to chase the dog, one to aid and comfort the sick man. But no dog was there, nor did he need comfort more. He had died with that cry on his lips, and as they gazed at his face, sunk low now in his pillow as if he had started up and fallen back, a dead weight, they felt the terror of the moment grow upon them till they, too, were speechless. For the aged features were drawn into lines of unspeakable anguish and horror.

But as the night passed and morning came, all these lines smoothed out, and when they buried him, those who had known him well talked of the beautiful serenity which illumined the face which, since their first remembrance of him, had carried the secret of a profound and unbroken melancholy. Of the dog, nothing was said, even in whispers, till time had hallowed that grave, and the little children about, grown to be men and women. Then the garrulity of age had its way.

This story, and the images it called up, came like a shock as I halted there, and instead of going on to the stables, I turned my steps toward the house, where I summoned from his bed a certain old servant who had lived longer in the family than myself.

Bidding him bring a lantern, I waited for him on the porch, and when he came, I told him what I had seen. Instantly I knew that it was no new story to him. He turned very pale and set down the lantern, which was shaking very visibly in his hand.

"Did you look up?" he asked; "when you were in the pavilion, I mean?"

"No; why should I? The dog was on the ground. Besides—"

"Let us go down to the pavilion," he whispered. "I want to see for myself if—if—"

"If what, Jared?"

He turned his eyes on me, but did not answer. Stooping, I lifted the lantern and put it in his hand. He was quaking like a leaf, but there was a determination in his face far beyond the ordinary. What made him quake—he who knew of this dog only by hearsay—and what, in spite of this fear, gave him such resolution? I followed in his wake to see what it was.

The moon still shone clear upon the lawn, and it was with a certain renewal of my former apprehensions that I approached the spot on the wall where I had seen what I was satisfied not to see again. But though I glanced that way—what man could have avoided it?—I perceived nothing but the bare paint, and we went on and passed in without a word, Jared leading the way.

But once on the threshold of the pavilion itself, it was for him to show the coward. Turning, he made me a gesture; one I did not understand; and seeing that I did not understand it, he said, after a fearful look around:

"Do not mind the dog; that was but an appearance. Lift your eyes to the ceiling—over there—at the extreme end toward the south—do you see—whatdo you see?"

"Nothing," I replied, amazed at what struck me as utter folly.

"Nothing?" he repeated in a relieved voice, as he lifted up his lantern. "Ah!" came in a sort of muttered shriek from his lips, as he pointed up, here and there, along the farther ceiling, over which the light now played freely and fully. "What is that spot, and that spot, and that? They were not there to-day. I was in here before the banquet, andIwould have seen. What is it? Master, what is it? They call it—"

"Well, well, what do they call it?" I asked impatiently.

"Blood! Do you not see that it is blood? What else is red and shiny and shows in such great drops—"

"Nonsense!" I vociferated, taking the lantern in my own hand. "Blood on the ceiling of my old pavilion? Where could it come from? There was no quarrel, no fight; only hilarity—"

"Where did the dog come from?" he whispered.

I dropped my arm, staring at him in mingled anger and a certain half-understood sympathy.

"You think these stains—" I began.

"Are as unreal as the dog? Yes, master."

Feeling as if I were in a dream, I tossed up the lantern again. The drops were still there, but no longer single or scattered. From side to side, the ceiling at this one end of the building oozed with the thick red moisture to which he had given so dreadful a name.

Stepping back for fear the stains would resolve themselves into rain and drop upon my forehead, I stared at Jared, who had now retreated toward the door.

"What makes you think it blood?" I demanded.

"Because some have smelt and tasted it. We have never talked about it, but this is not an uncommon occurrence. To-morrow all these stains will be gone. They come when the dog circles the wall. Whence, no one knows. It is our mystery. All the old servants have heard of it more than once. The new ones have never been told. Nor would I have told you if you had not seen the dog. It was a matter of honor with us."

I looked at him, saw that he believed every word he said, threw another glance at the ceiling, and led the way out. When we had reached the house again, I said:

"You are acquainted with the tradition underlying these appearances, as you call them. What is it?"

He could not tell me. He knew no more than he had already stated—gossip and old wives' tales. But later, a certain manuscript came into my possession through my lawyer, which I will append to this.

It was written by my unhappy father, some little time before his last illness, and given into the charge of the legal representative of our family, with the express injunction that its seal was to remain intact if for twenty years the apparition which had haunted him did not present itself to the eyes of any of his children. But if within that time his experience should repeat itself in theirs, this document was to be handed over to the occupant of Homewood. Nineteen out of the twenty years had elapsed, without the dog being seen or the ceiling of the pavilion dropping blood. But not the twentieth; hence, the document was mine.

You can easily conceive with what feelings I opened it. It was headed with this simple line:

MY STORY WHICH I CAN WRITE
BUT COULD NEVER TELL.

I am cursed with an inability to speak when I am most deeply moved, either by anger or tenderness. This misfortune has wrecked my life. On the verge of old age, the sorrows and the mistakes of my early life fill my thoughts so completely that I see but one face, hear but one voice; yet when she was living—whenshecould see and hear, my tongue was silent and she never knew. Aline! my Aline!

I married her when I was thirty-five and she eighteen. All the world knows this; but what it does not know is that I loved her—toy, plaything that she was—a body without a mind—(or, so I considered her)—while she had but followed the wishes of her relatives in giving her sweet youth to a cold and reticent man who might love, indeed, but who had no power to tell that love, or even to show it in the ways which women like, and which she liked, as I found out when it was too late.

I could not help but love her. It was ingrained within me; a part of the curse of my life to love this gentle, thoughtless, alluring thing to which I had given my name. She had a smile—it did not come often—which tore at my heart-strings as it welled up, just stirring the dimples in her cheeks, and died away again in a strange and moving sweetness. Though I reckoned her at her worth; knew that her charm was all physical; that she neither did nor could understand a passion like mine, much less return it, it was none the less irresistible, and I have known myself to stand before a certain book-shelf in the turn of the stairway for many minutes together, because I knew that she would soon be coming down, and that, when she did, some ribbon from her gown would flutter by me, and I should feel the soft contact and go away happy to my books. Yet, if she stopped to look back at me, I could only return her look with one she doubtless called harsh, for she had not eyes to see below the surface.

I tell you all this, lest you may not understand. She was not your mother and you may begrudge me the affection I felt for her; if so, thrust these leaves into the fire and seek not the explanation of what has surprised you; for there is no word written here which does not find its meaning in the intense love I bore for her, my young girl-wife, and the tragedy which this love has brought into my life. She was slight in body, slight in mind and of slight feeling. I first discovered this last on the day I put my mother's ring on her finger. She laughed as I fitted it close and kissed the little hand. Not from embarrassment or childish impulse; I could have understood that; but indifferently, like one who did not know and never could. Yet I married her, and for six months lived in a fool's paradise. Then came that hall. It was held near here, very near, at one of our neighbor's, in fact. I remember that we walked, and that, coming to the driveway, I lifted her and carried her across. Not with a smile—do not think it. More likely with a frown, though my heart was warm and happy; for when I set her down, she shook herself, and I thought she did it to hide a shudder, and then I could not have spoken a word had my life depended on it.

I little knew what lay back of that shudder. Even after I had seen her dance with him, not only once, but twice, I never dreamed that her thoughts, light though they were, were not all with me. It took that morsel of paper and the plain words it contained to satisfy me of this, and then— But passion is making me incoherent. What do you know of that scrap of paper, hidden from the whole world from the moment I first read it till this hour of full confession? It fluttered from some one's hand during the dance. I did not see whose. I only saw it after it had fallen at my feet, and as it lay there open I naturally read the words. They were written by a man to a woman, urging flight and setting the hour and place for meeting. I was conscious of shame in reading it, and let these last details escape me. As I put it in my pocket I remember thinking, "Some poor devil made miserable!" for there had been hint in it of the husband. But I had no thought—I swear it before God—of who that husband was till I beheld her flit back through the open doorway, with terror in her mien and searching eyes fixed on the floor. Then hell opened before me, and I saw my happiness go down into gulfs I had never before sounded, even in imagination.

But even at that evil hour my countenance scarcely changed—I was opposite a mirror, and I caught a glimpse of myself as I moved. But there must have been some change in my voice—for when I addressed her, she started and turned her face upon me with a wild and pathetic look which knocked so at my heart that I wished I had never read those words, and so could return her the paper with no misgiving as to its contents. But having read it, I could not do this; so, beyond a petty greeting, I said nothing and let the moment pass, and she with it; for couples were dancing and she was soon again in the whirl. I am not a dancing man myself, and I had leisure to think and madden myself with contemplation of my wrecked life and questions as to what I should do to her and to him, and to the world where such things could happen. I had forgotten the details of time and place, or rather had put them out of my mind, and I would not look at the words again—could not. But as the minutes went by, the remembrance returned, startling and convincing, that the hour was two and the place—our old pavilion.

I walked about after that like a man in whose breast the sources of life are frozen. I chatted—I who never chatted—with women, and with men. I even smiled—once. That was when my little white-faced wife asked me if it were not time to go home. Even a man under torture might find strength to smile if the inquisitor should ask if he were not ready to be released.

And we went home.

I did not carry her this time across the driveway; but when we parted in the library, where I always spent an hour before retiring, I picked out a lily from a vase of flowers standing on my desk and held it out to her. She stared at it for a moment, quite as white as the lily, then she slowly put out her hand and took it. I felt no mercy after that, and bade her good-night with the remark that I should have to write far into the morning, and that she need not worry over my light, which I should not probably put out till she was half through with her night's rest.

For answer, she dropped the lily. I found it next morning lying withered and brown, in the hall-way.

That light did burn far into the morning; but I was not there to trim it. Before the fatal hour had struck, I had left the house and made my way to the pavilion. As I crossed the sward I saw the gleam of a lantern at the masthead of a small boat riding near our own landing-place, and I understood where he was at this hour, and by what route he hoped to take my darling. "A route she will never travel," thought I, striving to keep out of my mind and conscience the vision of another route, another travel, which that sweet young body might take if my mood held and my purpose strengthened.

There was no moon that night, and the copse in which our pavilion stands was like a blot against the starless heavens. As I drew near it, my dog, the invariable companion of my walks, lifted a short, sharp bark from the stables. But I knew whose hand had fastened him, and I went on without giving him a thought. At the door of the pavilion I stopped. All was dark within as without, and the silence was something to overwhelm the heart. She was not there then, nor was he. But he would be coming soon, and up or down between the double hedge-rows.

I went to meet him. It was a small detail, but possibly a necessary one. In her eyes he was probably handsome and gifted with all that I openly lacked. But he was shallow and small for a man like me to be concerned about. I laughed inwardly and with very conceivable scorn as I heard the faint fall of his footsteps in the darkness. It was nearly two and he meant to be prompt.

Our coming together in that narrow path was very much what I expected it to be. I had put out my arms and touched the hedge on either side, so that he could not escape me. When I heard him drawing close, I found the voice I had not had for her, and observed very quietly and with the cold politeness of a messenger:

"My wife finds herself indisposed since the ball, and begs to be excused from joining you in the pleasant sail you proposed to her."

That, and no more; except that when he started and almost fell into my arms, I found strength to add:

"The wind blows fresh to-night; you will have no difficulty in leaving this shore. The difficulty will be to return."

I had no heart to kill him; he was young and he was frightened. I heard the sob in his throat as I dropped my arm and he went flying down to the river.

This was child's play; the rest—

My portion is to tell it; forty years ago it all befell, and till now no word of it has ever left my lips.

There was no sound of her advancing tread across the lawn as I stepped back into my own grounds to enter the pavilion. But as I left the path and put foot inside the wall, I heard a far, faint sound like the harsh closing of a door in timid hands, followed by another bark from the dog, louder and sharper than the first—for he did not recognize my Aline as mistress, though I had striven for six months to teach him the place she held in my heart.

By this I knew she was coming, and that what preparations I had to make must be made soon. They were not many. Entering the well-known place, I lit the lantern I had brought with me and set it down near the door. It cast a feeble light about the entrance, but left great shadows in the rear. This I had calculated on, and into these shadows I now stepped.

The pavilion, as you remember it, is not what it was then. I had used it little, fancying more my own library up at the house, but it was not utterly without furnishings, and to young eyes might even look attractive, with love, or fancied love, to mellow its harsh lines and lend romance to its solitude. At this hour and under these circumstances it was a dismal hole to me; and as I stood there waiting, I thought how the place fitted the deed—if deed it was to be.

I had always thought her timid, afraid of the night and all threatening things. But as I listened to the sound of her soft footfall at the door, I realized that even her breast could grow strong under the influence of a real or fancied passion. It was a shock—but I did not cry out—only set my teeth together and turned a little so that what light there was would fall on my form rather than on my face.

She entered; I felt rather than heard the tremulous push she gave to the door, and the quick drawing in of her breath as she put her foot across the threshold. These sapped my courage. This fear, this almost hesitation, drew me from thoughts of myself to thoughts of her, and it was in a daze of mingled purposes and regrets that I felt her at last at my side.

"Walter!" fell softly, doubtfully from her lips.

It was the name of him the dip of whose oars as he made for his boat I could now faintly hear in the river below us.

Turning, I looked her in the face.

"You are late," said I. God gave me words in my extremity. "Walter has gone." Then, as the madness of terror replaced love in her eyes, I lifted her forcibly and carried her to the window, where I drew aside the vines. "That is his boat's lantern you see drawing away from the dock. I bade him God-speed. He will not come again."

Without a word she looked, then fell back on my arm. It was not life which forsook her face, and left her whole sweet body inert—that I could have borne, for did she not merit death who had killed my love, killed me?—but happiness, the glow of youthful blood, the dreams of a youthful brain. And seeing this, seeing that the heart I thought a child's heart had gone down in this shipwreck, I felt my anger swell and master me body and soul, and before I knew it, I was towering over her and she was cowering at my feet, crushed and with hands held up in defense, hands that had been like rose-leaves in my grasp, futile hands, but raised now in entreaty for her life to me, to me who had loved her.

Why did they not move me? Why did my muscles tighten instead of relax? I do not know; I had never thought myself a cruel man, but at that instant I felt that this toy of my strong manhood had done harm far beyond its value, and that it would comfort me to break it and toss it far aside; only I could not bear the cry which now left her lips:

"I am so young! not yet, not yet, Philo! I am so young! Let me live a little while."

Was it a woman's plea, conscious of the tenderness she appealed to, or only a child's instinctive grasping after life, just life? If it were the first, it would be easy to finish; but a child's terror, a child's longing—that pulled hard at my manhood, and under the possibility, my own arm fell.

Instantly her head drooped. No defense did she utter; no further plea did she make; she simply waited.

"You have deserved death." This I managed to utter. "But if you will swear to obey me, you shall not pay your forfeit till you have had a further taste of life. Not in my house; there is not sufficient freedom within its walls for you; but in the broad world, where people dance and sing and grow old at their leisure, without duty and without care. For three months you shall have this, and have it to your heart's content. Then you shall come back to me my true wife, if your heart so prompts; if not, to tell me of your failure and quit me for ever. But—" Here I fear my voice grew terrible, for her hands instinctively rose again. "Those three months must be lived unstained. As you are in God's sight this hour, I demand of you to swear that, if you forget this or disregard it, or for any cause subject my name to dishonor, that you will return unbidden at the first moment your reason returns to you, to take what punishment I will. On this condition I send you away to-night. Aline, will you promise?"

She did not answer; but her face rose. I did not understand its look. There was pathos in it, and something else. That something else troubled me.

"Are you dissatisfied?" I asked. "Is the time too short? Do you want more months for dancing?"

She shook her head and the little hands rose again:

"Do not send me away," she faintly entreated; "I don't know why—but I—had rather stay."

"With me? Impossible. Are you ready to promise, Aline?"

Then she rose and looked me in the eye with courage, almost with resolution.

"As I live!" said she.

And I knew she would keep her word.

The next thing I remember of that night was the sight of her little white, shivering figure looking out at me from the carriage that was to carry her away. The night was cold, and I had tucked her in with as much care as I might have done the evening before, when I still worshiped her, still thought her mine, or at least as much mine as she was any one's. When I had done this and pressed a generous gift into her hand, I stood a minute at the carriage door, in pity of her aspect. She looked so pinched and pale, so dazed and hopeless. Had she been alone—but the companion with whom I had provided her was at her side and my tongue was tied. I turned, and the driver started up the horses.

"Philo!" I heard blown by me on the wind.

Was it she who called? No, for there was anguish in the cry, the anguish of a woman, and she was only a frightened, disheartened child whom I had sent away to—dance.

One month, two months went by, and I began to take up my life. Another, and she would be home for good or ill. I thought that I could live through that other. I had heard of her; not from her—that I did not require; and the stories were all of the same character. She was enjoying life in the great city to which I had sent her; radiant at night, if a little spiritless by day. She was at balls, at concerts and at theaters. She wore jewels and shone with the best; I might be proud of her conquests and the sweetness and dignity with which she bore herself. Thus her friends wrote.

But she wrote nothing; I had not required it. Once, some one—a visitor at the house—spoke of having seen her. "She was surrounded with admirers," he had said. "How early our American women ripen!" was his comment. "She held her head like one who has held sway for years; but I thought her a trifle worn; as if pleasure absorbed too much of her sleep. You must look out for her, Judge."

And I smiled grimly enough, I own, to think just how I was looking out for her.

Then came the thunderbolt.

"I am told that no one ever sees her in the day-time; that she is always busy, days. But she does not look as if she took that time for rest. What can your little wife be doing? You ought to hurry up that important opinion of yours and go see."

He was right; what was she doing? And why shouldn't I go see? There was no obstacle but my own will; but that is the greatest obstacle a man can have. I remained at Homewood, but the four weeks of our further probation looked like a year.

Meanwhile, I had my way with the pavilion. I have shown you my heart, sometimes at its best, oftenest at its worst. I will show it to you again in this. I had a wall built round it, close against the thicket in which it lay embedded. This wall was painted white, and near it I had lamps placed which were lit at nightfall. Should a figure pass that wall I could see it from my window. No one could enter that doorway now, without running the risk of my seeing him from where I sat at my desk.

Did I feel easier? I do not know that I did. I merely followed an impulse I dared not name to myself.

Two weeks of this final month went by. Then (it was in the evening) some one came running up from the grounds, with the message that Mrs. Ocumpaugh had ridden into the gate, but that she was not ready to enter the house. Would I meet her at the pavilion?

I was in the library, at my desk, with my eyes on the wall, when this was told me. I had just seen the fierce figure of that unmanageable dog of mine run by that white surface, and my lips were open to order him tied up, when he, and everything else in this whole world, was forgotten in this crushing news of her return. For the three months were not up and her presence here could mean but one thing—she had found temptation too much for her, and she had come back to tell me so in obedience to her promise.

"I will go meet Mrs. Ocumpaugh," I said.

The man stared.

"I will go meet Mrs. Ocumpaugh now," I repeated, and tried to rise.

But my limbs refused; death had entered my heart, and it was some few minutes before I found myself upon the lawn outside.

When I got there I was trembling and so uncertain of movement that I tottered at the gate. But seeing signs of her presence within, I straightened myself and went in.

"I SHOULD NOT HAVE KNOWN THE WOMAN WHO STOOD THERE WITH MY NAME FORMED ON HER LIPS."

She was standing at the extreme end of the room when I entered, in the full light of the solitary moonbeam which shot in at the western casement. She had thrown aside her hat and coat, and never in all my life had I seen anything so ethereal as the worn face and wasted form she thus disclosed. Had it not been for the haunting and pathetic smile which by some freak of fate gave poignancy to her otherwise infantile beauty, I should not have known the woman who stood there with my name formed on her lips.

"Destroyed!" was my thought; and the rage which I felt that moment against fate flushed my whole being, and my arms went up, not in threat against her, but to an avenging Heaven, when I heard an impetuous rush, an angry growl, and the delicate, trembling figure went down under the leap of the monstrous animal which I had taught to love me, but could never teach to love her.

In horror and unspeakable anguish of soul I called off the dog; and, stooping with bitter cries, I took her in my arms.

"Hurt?" I gasped. "Hurt, Aline?" I looked at her anxiously.

"No," she whispered, "happy." And before I realized my own feelings or the passion with which I drew her to my breast, she had nestled her head against my heart, smiled and died.

The shock of the dog's onslaught had killed her.

I would not believe it at first, but when I was quite sure, I took out the pistol I carried in my breast and shot the cowering brute midway between the eyes.

When this was done, I turned back to her. There was no light but the moon, and I needed no other. The clear beams falling on her face made her look pure and stainless and sweet. I could almost have loved her again as I marked the tender smile which lingered from that passing moment on her lips. "Happy," she had said. What did she mean by that "Happy"? As I asked myself I heard a cry. The companion who had been with her had rushed in at the doorway, and was gazing in sorrow and amazement at the white form lying outstretched and senseless against that farther wall.

"Oh," she cried, in a tone that assured me she had not seen the dog lying in his blood at my back; "dead already? dead at the first glance? at the first word? Ah, she knew better than I, poor lamb. I thought she would get well if she once got home. She wearied so for you, sir, and for Homewood!"

I thought myself quite mad; past understanding aright the words addressed to me.

"She wearied —" I began.

"With all her soul for you and Homewood," the young woman repeated. "That is, since her illness developed."

"Her illness?"

"Yes, she has been ill ever since she went away. The cold of that first journey was too much for her. But she kept up for several weeks — doing what no other woman ever did before with so little strength and so little hope. Danced at night and —"

"And — and — what by day, what?" I could hardly get the words out of my mouth.

"Studied. Learned what she thought you would like — French — music — politics. It was to have been a surprise. Poor soul! it took her very life. She did not sleep — Oh, sir, what is it?"

I was standing over her, probably a terrifying figure. Lights were playing before my eyes, strange sounds were in my ears, everything about me seemed resolving itself into chaos.

"What do you mean?" I finally gasped. "She studied — to pleaseme? Why did she come back, then, so soon — " I paused, choked. I had been about to give away my secret. "I mean, why did she come thus suddenly, without warning me of what I might expect? I would have gone — "

"I told her so; but she was very determined to come to you herself — to this very pavilion. She had set the time later, but this morning the doctor told her that her symptoms were alarming, and without consulting him or heeding the advice of any of us, she started for home. She was buoyant on the way, and more than once I heard her softly repeating your name. Her heart was very loving — Oh, sir, you are ill!"

"No, no," I cried, crushing my hand against my mouth to keep down the cry of anguish and despair which tore its way up from my heart. "Before other hands touch her, other eyes see her, tell me when she began — I will not say to love me, but to weary for me and — Homewood."

"Perhaps she has told you herself. Here is the letter, sir, she bade me give you if she did not reach here alive. She wrote it this morning, after the doctor told her what I have said."

"Give — give — "

She put it in my hand. I glanced at it in the moonlight, read the first few words, and felt the world reel round me. Thrusting the letter in my breast, I bade the woman, who watched me with fascinated eyes, to go now and rouse the house. When she was gone I stepped back into the shadows, and catching hold of the murderous beast, I dragged him out and about the wall to a thick clump of bushes. Here I left him and went back to my darling. When they came in, they found her in my arms. Her head had fallen back and I was staring, staring, at her white throat.

That night, when all was done for her which could be done, I shut myself into my library and again opened that precious letter. I give it, to show how men may be mistaken when they seek to weigh women's souls:

My Husband:

I love you. As I shall be dead when you read this, I may say so without fear of rebuff. I did not love you then; I did not love anybody; I was thoughtless and fond of pleasure, and craved affectionate words. He saw this and worked on my folly; but when his project failed and I saw his boat creep away, I found that what feeling I had was for the man who had thwarted him, and I felt myself saved.

If I had not taken cold that night I might have lived to prove this. I know that you do not love me very much, but perhaps you would have done so had you seen me grow a little wiser and more like what your wife should be. I was trying when—O Philo, I can not write—I can not think. I am coming to you—I love—forgive—and take me back again, alive or dead. I love you—I love—

As I finished, the light, which had been burning low, suddenly went out. The window which opened before me was still unshuttered. Before me, across the wide spaces of the lawn, shone the pavilion wall, white in the moonlight. As I stared in horror at it, a trembling seized my whole body, and the hair on my head rose. The dark figure of a running dog had passed across it—the dog which lay dead under the bushes.

"God's punishment," I murmured, and laid my head down on that pathetic letter and sobbed.

The morning found me there. It was not till later that the man sent to bury the dog came to me with the cry, "Something is wrong with the pavilion! When I went in to close the window I found the ceiling at that end of the room strangely dabbled. It looks like blood. And the spots grew as I looked."

Aghast, bruised in spirit and broken of heart, I went down, after that sweet body was laid in its grave, to look. The stains he had spoken of were gone. But I lived to see them reappear,—as you have.

God have mercy on our souls!

XII-BEHIND THE WALL

"A most pathetic and awesome history!" I exclaimed, after the pause which instinctively followed the completion of this tale, read as few of its kind have ever been read, by this woman of infinite resources in feeling and expression.

"Is it not? Do you wonder that a visit in the dead of night to a spot associated with such superstitious horrors should frighten me?" she added as she bundled up the scattered sheets with a reckless hand.

"I do not. I am not sure but that I am a little bit frightened myself," I smiled, following with my eye a single sheet which had escaped to the floor. "Allow me," I cried, stooping to lift it. As I did so I observed that it was the first sheet, the torn one—and that a line or so of writing was visible at the top which I was sure had not been amongst those she had read.

"What words are those?" I asked.

"I don't know, they are half gone as you can see. They have nothing to do with the story. I read you the whole of that."

Mistress as she was of her moods and expression I detected traces of some slight confusion.

"The putting up of the partition is not explained," I remarked.

"Oh, that was put up in horror of the stains which from time to time broke out on the ceiling at that end of the room."

I wished to ask her if this was her conclusion or if that line or two I have mentioned was more intelligible than she had acknowledged it to be. But I refrained from a sense of propriety.

If she appreciated my forbearance she did not show it. Rising, she thrust the papers into a cupboard, casting a scarcely perceptible glance at the clock as she did so.

I took the hint and rose. Instantly she was all smiles.

"You have forgotten something, Mr. Trevitt. Surely you do not intend to carry away with you my key to the bungalow."

"I was thinking of it," I returned lightly. "I am not quite through with that key." Then before she could recover from her surprise, I added with such suavity as I had been able to acquire in my intercourse with my more cultivated clients:

"I have to thank you, Mrs. Carew, for an hour of thrilling interest. Absorbed though I am in the present mystery, my mind has room for the old one. Possibly because there is sometimes a marked connection between old family events and new. There may be some such connection in this case. I should like the opportunity of assuring myself there is not."

She said nothing; I thought I understood why. More suavely yet, I continued, with a slight, a very slight movement toward the door: "Rarely have I had the pleasure of listening to such a tale read by such an interpreter. It will always remain in my memory, Mrs. Carew. But the episode is over and I return to my present duty and the bungalow."

"The bungalow! You are going back to the bungalow?"

"Immediately."

"What for? Didn't you see all there was to see?"

"Not quite."

"I don't know what there can be left."

"Nothing of consequence, most likely, but you can not wish me to have any doubts on the subject."

"No, no, of course not."

The carelessness of her tone did not communicate itself to her manner. Seeing that my unexpected proposition had roused her alarm, I grew wary and remarked:

"I was always overscrupulous."

With a lift of her shoulders—a dainty gesture which I congratulated myself I could see unmoved—she held out her hand in a mute appeal for the key, but seeing that I was not to be shaken in my purpose, reached for the wrap she had tossed on a chair and tied it again over her head.

"What are you going to do?" I asked.

"Accompany you," she declared.

"Again? I thought the place frightened you."

"It does," she replied. "I had rather visit any other spot in the whole world; but if it is your intention to go back there, it is mine to go with you."

"You are very good," I replied.

But I was seriously disconcerted notwithstanding. I had reckoned upon a quiet hour in the bungalow by myself; moreover, I did not understand her motive for never trusting me there alone. Yet as this very distrust was suggestive, I put a good face on the matter and welcomed her company with becoming alacrity. After all, I might gain more than I could possibly lose by having her under my eye for a little longer. Strong as was her self-control there were moments when the real woman showed herself, and these moments were productive.

As we were passing out she paused to extinguish a lamp which was slightly smoking, — I also thought she paused an instant to listen. At all events her ears were turned toward the stairs down which there came the murmur of two voices, one of them the little boy's.

"It is time Harry was asleep," she cried. "I promised to sing to him. You won't be long, will you?"

"You need not be very long," was my significant retort. "I can not speak for myself."

Was I playing with her curiosity or anxieties or whatever it was that affected her? I hardly knew; I spoke as impulse directed and waited in cold blood — or was it hot blood? — to see how she took it.

Carelessly enough, for she was a famous actress except when taken by surprise. Checking an evident desire of calling out some direction up stairs, she followed me to the door, remarking cheerfully, "You can not be very long either; the place is not large enough."

My excuse — or rather the one I made to myself for thus returning to a place I had seemingly exhausted, was this. In the quick turn I had made in leaving on the former occasion, my foot had struck the edge of the large rug nailed over the center of the floor, and unaccountably loosened it. To rectify this mishap, and also to see how so slight a shock could have lifted the large brass nails by which it had been held down to the floor, seemed reason enough for my action. But how to draw her attention to so insignificant a fact without incurring her ridicule I could not decide in our brief passage back to the bungalow, and consequently was greatly relieved when, upon opening the door and turning my lantern on the scene, I discovered that in our absence the rug had torn itself still farther free from the floor and now lay with one of its corners well curled over — the corner farthest from the door and nearest the divan where little Gwendolen had been lying when she was lifted and carried away — where?

Mrs. Carew saw it too and cast me a startled look which I met with a smile possibly as ambiguous as the feeling which prompted it.

"Who has been here?" she asked.

"Ourselves."

"Did we do that?"

"I did; or rather my foot struck the edge of the rug as I turned to go out with you. Shall I replace it and press back the nails?"

"If you will be so good."

Do what she would there was eagerness in her tone. Remarking this, I decided to give another and closer look at the floor and the nails. I found the latter had not been properly inserted; or rather that there were two indentations for every nail, a deep one and one quite shallow. This caused me to make some examination of the others, those which had not been drawn from the floor, and I found that one or two of them were equally insecure, but not all; only those about this one corner.

Mrs. Carew, who had paused, confused and faltering in the doorway, in her dismay at seeing me engaged in this inspection instead of in replacing the rug as I had proposed, now advanced a step, so that our glances met as I looked up with the remark:

"This rug seems to have been lately raised at this corner. Do you know if the police had it up?"

"I don't. I believe so—oh, Mr. Trevitt," she cried, as I rose to my feet with the corner of the rug in my hand, "what are you going to do?"

She had run forward impetuously and was now standing close beside me—inconveniently close.

"I am going to raise this rug," I informed her. "That is, just at this corner. Pardon me, I shall have to ask you to move."

"Certainly, of course," she stammered. "Oh, what is going to happen now?" Then as she watched me: "There is—thereissomething under it. A door in the floor—a—a—Mrs. Ocumpaugh never told me of this."

"Do you suppose she knew it?" I inquired, looking up into her face, which was very near but not near enough to be in the full light of the lantern, which was pointed another way.

"This rug appears to have been almost soldered to the floor, everywhere but here. There! it is thrown back. Now, if you will be so very good as to hold the lantern, I will try and lift up the door."

"I can not. See, how my hands shake! What are we about to discover? Nothing, I pray, nothing. Suspense would be better than that."

"I think you will be able to hold it," I urged, pressing the lantern upon her.

"Yes; I have never been devoid of courage. But—but—don't ask me to descend with you," she prayed, as she lifted the lantern and turned it dexterously enough on that portion of the door where a ring lay outlined in the depths of its outermost plank.

"I will not; but you will come just the same; you can not help it," I hazarded, as with the point of my knife-blade I lifted the small round of wood which filled into the ring and thus made the floor level.

"Now, if this door is not locked, we will have it up," I cried, pulling at the ring with a will. The door was not locked and it came up readily enough, discovering some half-dozen steps, down which I immediately proceeded to climb.

"Oh, I can not stay here alone," she protested, and prepared to follow me in haste just as I expected her to do the moment she saw the light withdrawn.

"Step carefully," I enjoined. "If you will honor me with your hand—" But she was at my side before the words were well out.

"What is it? What kind of place do you make it out to be; and is there anything here you—do—not—want—to see?"

I flashed the light around and incidentally on her. She was not trembling now. Her cheeks were red, her eyes blazing. She was looking at me, and not at the darksome place about her. But as this was natural, it being a woman's way to look for what she desires to learn in the face of the man who for the moment is her protector, I shifted the light into the nooks and corners of the low, damp cellar in which we now found ourselves.

"Bins for wine and beer," I observed, "but nothing in them." Then as I measured the space before me with my eye, "It runs under the whole house. See, it is much larger than the room above."

"Yes," she mechanically repeated.

I lowered the lantern to the floor but quickly raised it again.

"What is that on the other side?" I queried. "I am sure there is a break in the wall over in that corner."

"I can not see," she gasped; certainly she was very much frightened. "Are you going to cross the floor?"

"Yes; and if you do not wish to follow me, sit down on these steps—"

"No, I will go where you go; but this is very fearful. Why, what is the matter?"

I had stepped aside in order to avoid a trail of footprints I saw extending across the cellar floor.

"Come around this way," I urged. "If you will follow me I will keep you from being too much frightened."

She did as I told her. Softly her steps fell in behind mine, and thus with wary tread and peering eyes we made our way to the remote end, where we found—or rather where I found—that the break which I had noticed in the uniformity of the wall was occasioned by a pile of old boxes, arranged so as to make steps up to a hole cut through the floor above.

With a sharp movement I wheeled upon her.

"Do you see that?" I asked, pointing back over my shoulder.

"Steps," she cried, "going up into that part of the building where—where—"

"Will you attempt them with me? Or will you stay here, in the darkness?"

"I—will—stay—here."

It was said with shortened breath; but she seemed less frightened than when we started to cross the cellar. At all events a fine look of daring had displaced the tremulous aspect which had so changed the character of her countenance a few minutes before.

"I will make short work of it," I assured her as I hastily ran up the steps. "Drop your face into your hands and you will not be conscious of the darkness. Besides, I will talk to you all the time. There! I have worked my way up through the hole. I have placed my lantern on the floor above and I see— What! are you coming?"

"Yes, I am coming."

Indeed, she was close beside me, maintaining her footing on the toppling boxes by a grip on my disengaged arm.

"Can you see?" I asked. "Wait! let me pull you up; we might as well stand on the floor as on these boxes."

Climbing into the room above, I offered her my hand, and in another moment we stood together in the noisome precincts of that abominable spot, with whose doleful story she had just made me acquainted.

A square of impenetrable gloom confronted me at the first glance — what might not be the result of a second?

I turned to consult the appearance of the lady beside me before I took this second look. Had she the strength to stand the ordeal? Was she as much moved — or possibly more moved than myself? As a woman, and the intimate friend of the Ocumpaughs, she should be. But I could not perceive that she was. For some reason, once in view of this mysterious place, she was strangely, inexplicably, impassibly calm.

"You can bear it?" I queried.

"I must — only end it quickly."

"I will," I replied, and I held out my lantern.

I am not a superstitious man, but instinctively I looked up before I looked about me. I have no doubt that Mrs. Carew did the same. But no stains were to be seen on those blackened boards now; or rather, they were dark with one continuous stain; and next moment I was examining with eager scrutiny the place itself.

Accustomed to the appearance of the cheerful and well-furnished room on the other side of the partition, it was a shock to me (I will not say what it was to her) to meet the bare decaying walls and mouldering appurtenances of this dismal hole. True, we had just come from a description of the place in all the neglect of its many years of desolation, yet the smart finish of the open portion we had just left poorly prepared us for what we here encountered.

But the first impression over — an impression which was to recur to me many a night afterward in dreams — I remembered the nearer and more imperative cause which had drawn us thither, and turning the light into each and every corner, looked eagerly for what I so much dreaded to find.

A couch to which some old cushions still clung stood against the farther wall. Thank God! it was empty; so were all the corners of the room. Nothing living and — nothing dead!

Turning quickly upon Mrs. Carew, I made haste to assure her that our fears were quite unfounded.

But she was not even looking my way. Her eyes were on the ground, and she seemed merely waiting — in some impatience, evidently, but yet merely waiting — for me to finish and be gone.

This was certainly odd, for the place was calculated in itself to rouse curiosity, especially in one who knew its story. A table, thick with dust and blurred with dampness, still gave tokens of a bygone festivity—among which a bottle and some glasses stood conspicuous. Cards were there too, dingy and green with mould—some on the table—some on the floor; while the open lid of a small desk pushed up close to a book-case full of books, still held a rusty pen and the remnants of what looked like the mouldering sheets of unused paper. As for the rest—desolation, neglect, horror—but nochild.

The relief was enormous.

"It is a dreadful place," I exclaimed; "but it might have been worse. Do you want to see things nearer? Shall we cross the floor?"

"No, no. We have not found Gwendolen; let us go. Oh, let us go!"

A thrill of feeling had crept into her voice. Who could wonder? Yet I was not ready to humor her very natural sensibilities by leaving quite so abruptly. The floor interested me; the cushions of that old couch interested me; the sawn boards surrounding the hole—indeed, many things.

"We will go in a moment," I assured her; "but, first, cast your eyes along the floor. Don't you see that some one has preceded us here; and that not so very long ago? Some one with dainty feet and a skirt that fell on the ground; in short, a woman and—a lady!"

"I don't see," she faltered, very much frightened; then quickly: "Show me, show me."

I pointed out the marks in the heavy dust of the long neglected floor; they were unmistakable.

"Oh!" she cried, "what it is to be a detective! But who could have been here? Who would want to be here? I think it is horrible myself, and if I were alone I should faint from terror and the close air."

"We will not remain much longer," I assured her, going straight to the couch. "I do not like it either, but—"

"What have you found now?"

Her voice seemed to come from a great distance behind me. Was this on account of the state of her nerves or mine? I am willing to think the latter, for at that moment my eye took in two unexpected details. A dent as of a child's head in one of the mangy sofa-pillows and a crushed bit of colored sugar which must once have been a bit of choice confectionery.

"Some one besides a lady has been here," I decided, pointing to the one and bringing back the other. "See! this bit of candy is quite fresh. You must acknowledge that.Thiswas not walled up years ago with the rest of the things we see about us."

Her eyes stared at the sugary morsel I held out toward her in my open palm. Then she made a sudden rush which took her to the side of the couch.

"GWENDOLEN HERE?" SHE MOANED. "GWENDOLEN HERE?"

"Gwendolen here?" she moaned. "Gwendolen here?"

"Yes," I began; "do not—"

But she had already left the spot and was backing toward the opening up which we had come. As she met my eye she made a quick turn and plunged below.

"I must have air," she gasped.

With a glance at the floor over which she had so rapidly passed, I hastily followed her, smiling grimly to myself. Intentionally or unintentionally, she had by this quick passage to and fro effectually confused, if not entirely obliterated, those evidences of a former intrusion which, with misguided judgment, I had just pointed out to her. But recalling the still more perfect line of footprints left below to which I had not called her attention, I felt that I could afford to ignore the present mishap.

As I reached the cellar bottom I called to her, for she was already half-way across.

"Did you notice where the boards had been sawed?" I asked. "The sawdust is still on the floor, and it smells as fresh as if the saw had been at work there yesterday."

"No doubt, no doubt," she answered back over her shoulder, still hurrying on so that I had to run lest she should attempt the steps in utter darkness.

When I reached the floor of the bungalow she was in the open door panting. Watching her with one eye, I drew back the trap into place and replaced the rug and the three nails I had loosened. Then I shut the slide of the lantern and joined her where she stood.

"Do you feel better?" I asked. "It was a dismal quarter of an hour. But it was not a lost one."

She drew the door to and locked it before she answered; then it was with a question.

"What do you make of all this, Mr. Trevitt?"

I replied as directly as the circumstances demanded.

"Madam, it is a startling answer to the question you put me before we first left your house. You asked then if the child in the wagon was Gwendolen. How could it have been she with this evidence before us of her having been concealed here at the very time that wagon was being driven away from—"

"I do not think you have reason enough—" she began and stopped, and did not speak again till we halted at the foot of her own porch. Then with the frank accent most in keeping with her general manner, however much I might distrust both accent and manner, she added as if no interval had intervened: "If those signs you noted are proofs to you that Gwendolen was shut up in that walled-off portion of the bungalow while some were seeking her in the water and others in the wagon, then where is she now?"

XIII-"WE SHALL HAVE TO BEGIN AGAIN"

It was a leading question which I was not surprised to see accompanied by a very sharp look from beneath the cloudy wrap she had wound about her head.

"You suspect some one or something," continued Mrs. Carew, with a return of the indefinable manner which had characterized her in the beginning of our interview. "Whom? What?"

I should have liked to answer her candidly, and in the spirit, if not the words, of the prophet of old, but her womanliness disarmed me. With her eyes on me I could get no further than a polite acknowledgment of defeat.

"Mrs. Carew, I am all at sea. We shall have to begin again."

"Yes," she answered like an echo—was it sadly or gladly?—"you will have to begin again." Then with a regretful accent: "And I can not help you, for I am going to sail to-morrow. I positively must go. Cablegrams from the other side hurry me. I shall have to leave Mrs. Ocumpaugh in the midst of her distress."

"What time does your steamer sail, Mrs. Carew?"

"At five o'clock in the afternoon, from the Cunard docks."

"Nearly sixteen hours from now. Perhaps fate—or my efforts—will favor us before then with some solution of this disheartening problem. Let us hope so."

A quick shudder to hide which she was reaching out her hand, when the door behind us opened and a colored girl looked out. Instantly and with the slightest possible loss of self-possession Mrs. Carew turned to motion the intruder back, when the girl suddenly blurted out:

"Oh, Mrs. Carew, Harry is so restless. He is sleepy, he says."

"I will be up instantly. Tell him that I will be up instantly." Then as the girl disappeared, she added, with a quick smile: "You see I haven't any toys for him. Not being a mother I forgot to put them in his trunk."

As though in response to these words the maid again showed herself in the doorway. "Oh, Mrs. Carew," she eagerly exclaimed, "there's a little toy in the hall here, brought over by one of Mrs. Ocumpaugh's maids. The girl said that hearing that the little boy fretted, Mrs. Ocumpaugh had picked out one of her little girl's playthings and sent it over with her love. It's a little horse, ma'am, with curly mane and a long tail. I am sure 'twill just please Master Harry."

Mrs. Carew turned upon me a look brimming with feeling.

"What thoughtfulness! What self-control!" she cried. "Take up the horse, Dinah. It was one of Gwendolen's favorite playthings," she explained to me as the girl vanished.

I did not answer. I was hearing again in my mind that desolate cry of "Philo! Philo! Philo!" which an hour or so before had rung down to me from Mrs. Ocumpaugh's open window. There had been a wildness in the tone, which spoke of a tossing head on a feverish pillow. Certainly an irreconcilable picture with the one just suggested by Mrs. Carew of the considerate friend sending out the toys of her lost one to a neighbor's peevish child.

Mrs. Carew appeared to notice the pre-occupation with which I lingered on the lower step.

"You like children," she hazarded. "Or have you interested yourself in this matter purely from business reasons?"

"Business reasons were sufficient," was my guarded reply. "But I like children very much. I should be most happy if I could see this little Harry of yours nearer. I have only seen him from a distance, you know."

She drew back a step; then she met my look squarely in the moonlight. Her face was flushed, but I attempted no apology for a presumption which could have but one excuse. I meant that she should understand me if I did not her.

"You must love children," she remarked, but not with her usual correctness of tone. Then before I could attempt an answer to the implied sarcasm a proud light came into her eyes, and with a gracious bend of her fine figure she met my look with one equally as frank, and cheerfully declared:

"You shall. Come early in the morning."

In another moment she had vanished inside and closed the door. I was defeated for the nonce, or else she was all she appeared to be and I a dreaming fool.

XIV-ESPIONAGE

As I moved slowly away into the night the question thus raised in my own mind assumed greater and more vital consequence. Was she a true woman or what my fears pictured her—the scheming, unprincipled abductor of Gwendolen Ocumpaugh? She looked true, sometimes acted so; but I had heard and seen what would rouse any man's suspicions, and though I was not in a position to say: "Mrs. Carew, this was not your first visit to that scene of old tragedy. You have been there before, and with Gwendolen in your arms," I was morally certain that this was so; that Mrs. Ocumpaugh's most trusted friend was responsible for the disappearance of her child, and I was not quite sure that the child was not now under her very roof.

It was very late by this time, but I meant, if possible, to settle some of these doubts before I left the neighborhood of the cottage.

How? By getting a glimpse of Mrs. Carew with her mask off; in the company of the child, if I could compass it; if not, then entirely alone with her own thoughts, plans and subtleties.

It was an act more in line with my partner's talents than my own, but I could not afford to let this deter me. I had had my chance with her, face to face. For hours I had been in her company. I had seen her in various stages of emotion, sometimes real and sometimes assumed, but at no moment had I been sure of her, possibly because at no moment had she been sure of me. In our first visit to the bungalow; in her own little library, during the reading of that engrossing tale by which she had so evidently attempted to lull my suspicions awakened by her one irrepressible show of alarm on the scene of Gwendolen's disappearance, and afterward when she saw that they might be so lulled but not dispelled; in the cellar; and, above all, in that walled-off room where we had come across the signs of Gwendolen's presence, which even she could not disavow, she had felt my eyes upon her and made me conscious that she had so felt them. Now she must believe them removed, and if I could but gain the glimpse I speak of I should see this woman as she was.

I thought I could manage this.

I had listened to the maid's steps as she returned up stairs, and I believed I knew in what direction they had tended after she reached the floor above. I would just see if one of the windows on the south side was lighted, and, if so, if it was in any way accessible.

To make my way through the shrubbery without rousing the attention of any one inside or out required a circumspection that tried me greatly. But by dint of strong self-control I succeeded in getting to the vantage-place I sought, without attracting attention or causing a single window to fly up. This reassured me, and perceiving a square of light in the dark mass of wall before me I peered about among the trees overlooking this part of the building for one I could climb without too much difficulty.

The one which looked most feasible was a maple with low-growing-branches, and throwing off my coat I was soon half-way to its top and on a level, or nearly so, with the window on which I had fixed my eye.

There were no curtains to this window — the house being half dismantled in anticipation of Mrs. Carew's departure — but it was still protected by a shade, and this was drawn down, nearly to the ledge.

But not quite. A narrow space intervened which, to an eye placed where mine was, offered a peep-hole of more or less satisfactory proportions, and this space, I soon saw, widened perceptibly from time to time as the wind caught at the shade and blew it in.

With utmost caution I shifted my position till I could bring my eye fairly in line with the interior of this room, and finding that the glimpse given revealed little but a blue wall and some snowy linen, I waited for the breeze to blow that I might see more.

It came speedily, and in a gust which lifted the shade and thus disclosed the whole inside of the room. It was an instantaneous glimpse, but in that moment the picture projected upon my eye satisfied me that, despite my doubts, despite my causes for suspicion, I had been doing this woman the greatest injustice in supposing that her relations to the child she had brought into her home were other than she had made out.

She had come up as she had promised, and had seated herself on the bed with her face turned toward the window. I could thus catch its whole expression — an expression this time involuntary and natural as the feelings which prompted it. The child, with his newly-obtained toy clutched in one hand, knelt on the coverlet with his head pressed against her breast, saying his prayers. I could hear his soft murmur, though I could not catch the words.

But sweet as was the sight of his little white-clad form burying its head, with its mass of dusky curls, against the breast in which he most confided, it was not this alone which gave to the moment its almost sacred character. It was the rapturous look with which Mrs. Carew gazed down on this little head — the mother-look, which admits of nothing false, and which when once seen on a woman's face, whether she be mother in fact or mother only in heart — idealizes her in the mind for ever.

Eloquent with love and holy devotion the scene flashed upon my eyes for a moment and was gone. But that moment made its impression, and settled for good and all the question with which I had started upon this adventure. Shewasthe true woman and I was the dreaming fool.

As I realized this I also realized that three days out of the seven were gone.

XV-A PHANTASM

I certainly had every right to conclude that this would end my adventures for the day. But I soon found that I was destined to have yet another experience before returning to my home in New York.

The weather had changed during the last hour and at the moment I emerged from the shadows of the hedge-row into the open space fronting the Ocumpaugh dock, a gleam of lightning shot across the west and by it I saw what looked like the dusky figure of a man leaning against a pile at the extreme end of the boat-house. Something in the immobility maintained by this figure in face of the quick flashes which from time to time lit up the scene, reminded me of the presence I had come upon hours before in front of Mrs. Carew's house; and moved by the instinct of my calling, I took advantage of the few minutes yet remaining before train time, to make my way in its direction, cautiously, of course, and with due allowance for the possible illumination following those fitful bursts of light which brought everything to view in one moment, only to plunge it all back into the profoundest obscurity the next.

I had two motives for my proceeding. One, as I say, sprang from the natural instinct of investigation; the other was kindlier and less personal.

I did not understand the meaning of the posture which this person had now assumed; nor did I like it. Why should this man—why should any man stand like this at the dead of night staring into waters, which, if they had their tale to tell, had not yet told it—unless his interest in the story he read there was linked with emotions such as it was my business to know? For those most openly concerned in Gwendolen's loss, the search had ceased; why, then, this lone and lingering watch on the part of one who might, for all I knew, be some over-zealous detective, but who I was rather inclined to believe was a person much more closely concerned in the child's fate, viz: the next heir-in-law, Mr. Rathbone. If it were he, his presence there savored of mystery or it savored of the tragic. The latter seemed the more likely hypothesis, judging from the expression of his face, as seen by me under the lantern. It behooved me then to approach him, but to approach him in the shadow of the boat-house.

What passed in the next few minutes seemed to me unreal and dreamlike. I was tired, I suppose, and so more than usually susceptible. Night had no unfamiliar effects for me, even night on the borders of this great river; nor was my occupation a new one, or the expectation I felt, as fearful and absorbing as that with which an hour or two before I had raised my lantern in that room in which the doleful mystery of half a century back, trenched upon the still more moving mystery of to-day. Yet, that experience had the sharpness of fact; while this had only the vagueness of a phantasm.

I was very near him but the lightning had ceased to flash, and I found it impossible to discern whether or not the form I had come there to identify, yet lingered in its old position against the pile.

I therefore awaited the next gleam with great anxiety, an anxiety only partly alleviated by the certainty I felt of hearing the faint, scarcely recognizable sound of his breathing. Had the storm passed over? Would no more flashes come? Ah, he is moving—that is a sigh I hear—no detective's exclamation of impatience, but a sufferer's sigh of depression or remorse. What was in the man's mind?

A steamboat or some equally brilliantly illuminated craft was passing, far out in the channel; the shimmer of its lights gave sudden cheer to the distant prospect; the churning of its paddles suggested life and action and irresistibly drew my eyes that way. Would his follow? Would I find his attitude changed?

Ah! the long delayed flash has come and gone. He is standing there yet, but no longer in an attitude of contemplation. On the contrary, he is bending over the waters searching with eager aspect, where so many had searched before him, and, in the instant, as his face and form leaped into sight, I beheld his clenched right hand fall on his breast and heard on his lips the one word—

"Guilty!"

XVI-"AN ALL-CONQUERING BEAUTY"

I was one of the first to procure and read a New York paper next morning. Would I discover in the columns any hint of the preceding day's events in Yonkers, which, if known, must for ever upset the wagon theory? No, that secret was still my secret, only shared by the doctor, who, so far as I understood him, had no intention of breaking his self-imposed silence till his fears of some disaster to the little one had received confirmation. I had therefore several hours before me yet for free work.

The first thing I did was to hunt up Miss Graham.

She met me with eagerness; an eagerness I found it difficult to dispel with my disappointing news in regard to Doctor Pool.

"He is not the man," said I. "Can you think of any other?"

She shook her head, her large gray eyes showing astonishment and what I felt bound to regard as an honest bewilderment.

"I wish to mention a name," said I.

"One I know?" she asked.

"Yes."

"I know of no other person capable of wronging that child."

"You are probably right. But there is a gentleman—one interested in the family—a man with something to gain—"

"Mr. Rathbone? You must not mention him in any such connection. He is one of the best men I know—kind, good, and oh, so sensitive! A dozen fortunes wouldn't tempt a man of his stamp to do any one living a wrong, let alone a little innocent child."

"I know; but there are other temptations greater than money to some men; infinitely greater to one as sensitive as you say he is. What if he loved a woman! What if his only hope of winning her—"

"You must not think that of him," she again interposed. "Nothing could make a villain ofhim. I have seen him too many times in circumstances which show a man's character. He is good through and through, and in all that concerns Gwendolen, honorable to the core. I once saw him save her life at the risk of his own."

"You did? When? Years ago?"

"No, lately; within the last year."

"Tell me the circumstances."

She did. They were convincing. As I listened, the phantasm of the night before assumed fainter and fainter proportions. When she had finished I warmly remarked that I was glad to hear the story of so heroic an act.

And I was. Not that I ascribed too deep a significance to the word which had escaped Mr. Rathbone on the dock, but because I was glad to have my instinctive confidence in the man verified by facts.

It seemed to clear the way before me.

"Ellie," said I (it seemed both natural and proper to call her by that name now), "what explanation would you give if, under any circumstances (all circumstances are possible, you know), you heard this gentleman speak of feeling guilty in connection with Gwendolen Ocumpaugh?"

"I should have to know the circumstances," was her quiet answer.

"Let me imagine some. Say that it was night, late night, at an hour when the most hardened amongst us are in a peculiarly responsive condition; say that he had been spending hours near the house of the woman he had long loved but had quite despaired of winning in his greatly hampered condition, and with the fever of this longing upon him, but restrained by emotions the nature of which we can not surmise, had now found his way down to the river—to the spot where boats have clustered and men crouched in the gruesome and unavailing search we know of; say that he hung there long over the water, gazing down in silence, in solitude, alone, as he thought, with his own conscience and the suggestions offered by that running stream where some still think, despite facts, despite all the probabilities, that Gwendolen has found rest, and when his heart was full, should be seen to strike his breast and utter, with a quick turn of his face up the hill, this one word, 'Guilty'?"

"What would I think? This: That being overwrought by the struggle you mention (a struggle we can possibly understand when we consider the unavoidable consciousness which must be his of the great change which would be effected in all his prospects if Gwendolen should not be found), he gave the name of guilt to feelings which some would call simply human."

"Ellie, you are an oracle." This thought of hers had been my thought ever since I had had time really to reflect upon the matter. "I wonder if you will have an equally wise reply to give to my next question?"

"I can not say. I speak from intuition; I am not really wise."

"Intuition is above wisdom. Does your intuition tell you that Mrs. Carew is the true friend she professes to be to Mrs. Ocumpaugh?"

"Ah, that is a different thing!"

The clear brow I loved—there! how words escape a man!—lost its smoothness and her eyes took on a troubled aspect, while her words came slowly.

"I do not know how to answer that offhand. Sometimes I have felt that her very soul was knit to that of Mrs. Ocumpaugh, and again I have had my doubts. But never deep ones; never any such as would make it easy for me to answer the question you have just put me."

"Was her love for Gwendolen sincere?" I asked.

"Oh, yes; oh, yes. That is, I always thought so, and with no qualification, till something in her conduct when she first heard of Gwendolen's disappearance—I can not describe it—gave me a sense of disappointment. She was shocked, of course, and she was grieved, but not hopelessly so. There was something lacking in her manner—we all felt it; Mrs. Ocumpaugh felt it, and let her dear friend go the moment she showed the slightest inclination to do so."

"There were excuses for Mrs. Carew, just at that time," said I. "You forget the new interest which had come into her life. It was natural that she should be preoccupied."

"With thoughts of her little nephew?" replied Miss Graham. "True, true; but she had been so fond of Gwendolen! You would have thought— But why all this talk about Mrs. Carew? You don't believe—you surely can not believe—"

"That Mrs. Carew is a charming woman? Oh, yes, but I do. Mr. Rathbone shows good taste."

"Ah, is she the one?"

"Did you not know it?"

"No; yet I have seen them together many times. Now I understand much that has always been a mystery to me. He never pressed his suit; he loved, but never harassed her. Oh, he is a good man!" This with emphasis.

"Is she a good woman?"

Miss Graham's eyes suddenly fell, then rose again until they met mine fully and frankly.

"I have no reason," said she, "to believe her otherwise. I have never seen anything in her to hinder my esteem; only—"

"Finish that 'only.'"

"She does not appeal to me as many less gifted women do. Perhaps I am secretly jealous of the extreme fondness Gwendolen has always shown for her. If so, the fault is in me, not in her."

What I said in reply is not germane to this story.

After being assured by a few more discreet inquiries in some other perfectly safe quarters that Miss Graham's opinion of Mr. Rathbone was shared by those who best knew him, I returned to the one spot most likely to afford me a clue to, if no explanation of, this elusive mystery.

What did I propose to myself? First, to revisit Mrs. Carew and make the acquaintance of the boy Harry. I no longer doubted his being just what she called him, but she had asked me to call for this purpose and I had no excuse for declining the invitation, even if I had desired to do so. Afterward—but first let us finish with Mrs. Carew.

As she entered her reception-room that morning she looked so bright— that is, with the instinctive brightness of a naturally vivacious temperament— that I wondered if I had been mistaken in my thought that she had had no sleep all that night, simply because many of the lights in her house had not been put out till morning. But an inspection of her face revealed lines of care, which only her smile could efface, and she was not quite ready for smiles, affable and gracious as she showed herself.

Her first words, just as I expected, were:

"There is nothing in the papers about the child in the wagon."

"No; everything does not get into the papers."

"Will what we saw and what we found in the bungalow last night?"

"I hardly think so. That is our own special clue, Mrs. Carew—if it is a clue."

"You seem to regard it as such."

With a shrug I declared that we had come upon a mystery of some kind.

"But the child is not dead? That you feel demonstrated—or don't you?"

"As I said last night, I do not know what to think. Ah; is that the little boy?"

"Yes," she gaily responded, as the glad step of a child was heard descending the stairs. "Harry! come here, Harry!" she cried, with that joyous accent which a child's presence seems to call out in some women. "Here is a gentleman who would like to shake hands with you."

A sprite of a child entered; a perfect sunbeam irradiating the whole room. If, under the confidence induced by the vision I had had of him on his knees the night before, any suspicion remained in my mind of his being Gwendolen

Ocumpaugh in disguise, it vanished at sight of the fearless head, lifted high in boyish freedom, and the gay swish, swish of the whip in his nervous little hand.

"Harry is playing horse," he cried, galloping toward me in what he evidently considered true jockey style.

I made a gesture and stopped him.

"How do you do, little man? What did you say your name is?"

"Harry," this very stoutly.

"Harry what? Harry Carew?"

"No, Harry; just Harry."

"And how do you like it here?"

"I like it; I like it better than my old home."

"Where was your old home?"

"I don't know. I didn't like it."

"He was with uncongenial people, and he is very sensitive," put in Mrs. Carew, softly.

"I like it here," he repeated, "and I like the big ocean. I am going on the ocean. And I like horses. Get up, Dandy!" and he cracked his whip and was off again on his imaginary trot.

I felt very foolish over the doubts I had so openly evinced. This was not only a boy to the marrow of his bones, but he was, as any eye could see, the near relative she called him. In my embarrassment I rose; at all events I soon found myself standing near the door with Mrs. Carew.

"A fine fellow!" I enthusiastically exclaimed; "and startlingly like you in expression. He is your nephew, I believe?"

"Yes," she replied, somewhat wistfully I thought.

I felt that I should apologize for—well, perhaps for the change she must have discerned in my manner.

"The likeness caused me a shock. I was not prepared for it, I suppose."

She looked at me quite wonderingly.

"I have never heard any one speak of it before. I am glad that you see it." And she seemed glad, very glad.

But I know that for some reason she was gladder yet when I turned to depart. However, she did not hasten me.

"What are you going to do next?" she inquired, as she courteously led the way through the piles of heaped-up boxes and baskets, the number of which had rather grown than diminished since my visit the evening before. "Pardon my asking."

"Resort to my last means," said I. "See and talk with Mrs. Ocumpaugh."

An instant of hesitation on her part, so short, however, that I could hardly detect it, then she declared:

"But you can not do that."

"Why not?"

"She is ill; I am sure that they will let no one approach her. One of her maids was in this morning. She did not even ask me to come over."

"I am sorry," said I, "but I shall make the effort. The illness which affects Mrs. Ocumpaugh can be best cured by the restoration of her child."

"But you have not found Gwendolen?" she replied.

"No; but I have discovered footprints on the dust of the bungalow floor, and, as you know, a bit of candy which looks as if it had been crushed in a sleeping child's hand, and I am in need of every aid possible in order to make the most of these discoveries. They may point the way to Gwendolen's present whereabouts and they may not. But they shall be given every chance."

"Whoop! get up! get up!" broke in a childish voice from the upper landing.

"Am I not right?" I asked.

"Always; only I am sorry for Mrs. Ocumpaugh. May I tell you—" as I laid my hand upon the outer door-knob—"just how to approach her?"

"Certainly, if you will be so good."

"I would not ask for Miss Porter. Ask for Celia; she is Mrs. Ocumpaugh's special maid. Let her carry your message—if you feel that it will do any good to disturb her."

"Thank you; the recommendation is valuable. Good morning, Mrs. Carew. I may not see you again; may I wish you a safe journey?"

"Certainly; are we not almost friends?"

Why did I not make my bow and go? There was nothing more to be said—at least by me. Was I held by something in her manner? Doubtless, for while I was thus reasoning with myself she followed me out on to the porch, and with some remark as to the beauty of the morning, led me to an opening in the vines, whence a fine view could be caught of the river.

But it was not for the view she had brought me there. This was evident enough from her manner, and soon she paused in her observations on the beauties of nature, and with a strange ringing emphasis for which I was not altogether prepared, remarked with feeling:

"I may be making a mistake—I was always an unconventional woman—but I think you ought to know something of Mrs. Ocumpaugh's private history before you see her. It is not a common one—at least it has its romantic elements—and an acquaintance with some of its features is almost necessary to you if you expect to approach her on so delicate a matter with any hope of success. But perhaps you are better informed on this subject than I supposed? Detectives are a mine of secret intelligence, I am told; possibly you have already learned from some other source the story of her marriage and homecoming to Homewood and the peculiar circumstances of her early married life?"

"No," I disclaimed in great relief, and I have no doubt with unnecessary vivacity. "On the contrary, I have never heard anything said in regard to it."

"Would you like to? Men have not the curiosity of women, and I do not wish to bore you, but—I see that I shall not do that," she exclaimed. "Sit down, Mr. Trevitt; I shall not detain you long; I have not much time myself."

As she sank into a chair in saying this, I had no alternative but to follow her example. I took pains, however, to choose one which brought me into the shadow of the vines, for I felt some embarrassment at this new turn in the conversation, and was conscious that I should have more or less difficulty in hiding my only too intense interest in all that concerned the lady of whom we were speaking.

"Mrs. Ocumpaugh was a western woman," Mrs. Carew began softly; "the oldest of five daughters. There was not much money in the family, but she had beauty, a commanding, all-conquering beauty; not the beauty you see in her to-day, but that exquisite, persuasive loveliness which seizes upon the imagination as well as moves the heart. I have a picture of her at eighteen—but never mind that."

Was it affection for her friend which made Mrs. Carew's always rich voice so very mellow? I wished I knew; but I was successful, I think, in keeping that wish out of my face, and preserving my manner of the simply polite listener.

"Mr. Ocumpaugh was on a hunting trip," she proceeded, after a slight glance my way. "He had traveled the world over and seen beautiful women everywhere; but there was something in Marion Allison which he had found in no other, and at the end of their first interview he determined to make her his wife. A man of impulses, but also a man of steady resolution, Mr. Trevitt. Perhaps you know this?"

I bowed. "A strong man," I remarked.

"And a romantic one. He had this intention from the first, as I have said, but he wished to make himself sure of her heart. He knew how his advantages counted; how hard it is for a woman to disassociate the man from his belongings, and having a spirit of some daring, he resolved that this 'pearl of the west'—so I have heard him call her—should marry the man and not his money."

"Was he as wealthy then as now?"

"Almost. Possibly he was not quite such a power in the financial world, but he had Homewood in almost as beautiful a condition as now, though the new house was not put up till after his marriage. He courted her—not as the landscape painter of Tennyson's poem—but as a rising young business man who had made his way sufficiently to give her a good home. This home he did not have to describe, since her own imagination immediately pictured it as much below the one she lived in, as he was years younger than her hard-worked father. Delighted with this naïveté, he took pains not to disabuse her mind of the simple prospects with which she was evidently so well satisfied, and succeeded in marrying her and bringing her as far as our station below there, without her having the least suspicion of the splendor she was destined for. And now, Mr. Trevitt, picture, if you can, the scene of that first arrival. I have heard it described by him and I have heard it described by her. He was dressed plainly; so was she; and lest the surprise should come before the proper moment, he had brought her on a train little patronized by his friends. The sumptuousness of the solitary equipage standing at the depot platform must, in consequence, have struck her all the more forcibly, and when he turned and asked her if she did not admire this fine turn-out, you can imagine the lovely smile with which she acknowledged its splendor and then turned away to look up and down for the street-car she expected to take with him to their bridal home.

"He says that he caught her back with the remark that he was glad she liked it because it was hers and many more like it. But she insists that he did not say a word, only smiled in a way to make her see for whom the carriage door was being held open. Such was her entrance into wealth and love and alas! into trouble. For the latter followed hard upon the two first. Mr. Ocumpaugh's mother, who had held sway at Homewood for thirty years or more, was hard as the nether millstone. She was a Rathbone and had brought both wealth and aristocratic connections into the family. She had no sympathy for penniless beauties (she was a very plain woman herself) and made those first few years of her daughter-in-law's life as nearly miserable as any woman's can be who adores her husband. I have heard that it was a common experience for this sharp-tongued old lady to taunt her with the fact that she brought nothing into the family but herself—not even a towel; and when two years passed and no child came, the biting criticisms became so frequent that a cloud fell over the young wife's sensitive beauty, which no after happiness has ever succeeded in fully dispelling. Matters went better after Gwendolen came, but in reckoning up the possible defects in Mrs. Ocumpaugh's character you should never forget the twist that may have been given to it by that mother-in-law."

"I have heard of Madam Ocumpaugh," I remarked, rising, anxious to end an interview whose purport was more or less enigmatic to me.

"She is dead now—happily. A woman like that is accountable for much more than she herself ever realizes. But one thing she never succeeded in doing: she never shook Mr. Ocumpaugh's love for his wife or hers for him. Whether it was the result of that early romantic episode of which I have spoken, or whether their natures are peculiarly congenial, the bond between them has been one of exceptional strength and purity."

"It will be their comfort now," I remarked.

Mrs. Carew smiled, but in a dubious way that added to my perplexity and made me question more seriously than ever just what her motive had been in subjecting me to these very intimate reminiscences of one I was about to approach on an errand of whose purport she could have only a general idea.

Had she read my inmost soul? Did she wish to save her friend, or save herself, or even to save me from the result of a blind use of such tools as were the only ones afforded me? Impossible to determine. She was at this present moment, as she had always been, in fact, an unsolvable problem to me, and it was not at this hurried time and with such serious work before me that I could venture to make any attempt to understand her.

"You will let me know the outcome of your talk with Mrs. Ocumpaugh?" she cried, as I moved to the front of the porch.

It was for me to look dubious now. I could make no such promise as that.

"I will let you know the instant there is any good news," I assured her.

And with that I moved off, but not before hearing the peremptory command with which she entered the house:

"Now, Dinah, quick!"

Evidently, her preparations for departure were to be pushed.

XVII-IN THE GREEN BOUDOIR

So far in this narrative I have kept from the reader nothing but an old experience of which I was now to make use. This experience involved Mrs. Ocumpaugh, and was the cause of the confidence which I had felt from the first in my ability to carry this search through to a successful termination. I believed that in some secret but as yet undiscovered way, it offered a key to this tragedy. And I still believed this, little as I had hitherto accomplished and blind as the way continued to look before me.

Nevertheless, it was with anything but a cheerful heart that I advanced that morning through the shrubbery toward the Ocumpaugh mansion.

I dreaded the interview I had determined to seek. I was young, far too young, to grapple with the difficulties it involved; yet I saw no way of avoiding it, or of saving either Mrs. Ocumpaugh or myself from the suffering it involved.

Mrs. Carew had advised that I should first see the girl called Celia. But Mrs. Carew knew nothing of the real situation. I did not wish to see any girl. I felt that no such intermediary would answer in a case like this. Nor did I choose to trust Miss Porter. Yet to Miss Porter alone could I appeal.

The sight of a doctor's gig standing at the side door gave me my first shock. Mrs. Ocumpaugh was ill, then, really ill. Yet if I came to make her better? I stood irresolute till I saw the doctor come out; then I walked boldly up and asked for Miss Porter.

Just what Mrs. Carew had advised me not to do.

Miss Porter came. She recognized me, but only to express her sorrow that Mrs. Ocumpaugh was totally unfit to see any one to-day.

"Not if he brings news?"

"News?"

"I have news, but of a delicate nature. I should like the privilege of imparting the same to Mrs. Ocumpaugh herself."

"Impossible."

"Excuse me, if I urge it."

"She can not see you. The doctor who has just gone says that at all hazards she must be kept quiet to-day. Won't Mr. Atwater do? Is it—is it good news?"

"That, Mrs. Ocumpaugh alone can say."

"See Mr. Atwater; I will call him."

"I have nothing to say tohim."

"But—"

"Let me advise you. Leave it to Mrs. Ocumpaugh. Take this paper up to her—it is only a sketch—and inform her that the person who drew it has something of importance to say either to her or to Mr. Atwater, and let her decide which it shall be. You may, if you wish, mention my name."

"I do not understand."

"You hold my credentials," I said and smiled.

She glanced at the paper I had placed in her hand. It was a folded one, fastened something like an envelope.

"I can not conceive,—" she began.

I did not scruple to interrupt her.

"Mrs. Ocumpaugh has a right to the privilege of seeing what I have sketched there," I said with what impressiveness I could, though my heart was heavy with doubt. "Will you believe that what I ask is for the best and take this envelope to her? It may mean the ultimate restoration of her child."

"This paper?"

"Yes, Miss Porter."

She did not try to hide her incredulity.

"I do not see how a picture—yet you seem very much in earnest—and I know she has confidence in you, she and Mr. Ocumpaugh, too. I will take it to her if you can assure me that good will come of it and no more false hopes to destroy the little courage she has left."

"I can not promise that. I believe that she will wish to receive me and hear all I have to say after seeing what that envelope contains. That is as far as I can honestly go."

"It does not satisfy me. If it were not for the nearness of Mr. Ocumpaugh's return, I would have nothing to do with it. He must hear at Sandy Hook that some definite news has been received of his child."

"You are right, Miss Porter, he must."

"He idolized Gwendolen. He is a man of strong feelings; very passionate and much given to follow the impulse of the moment. If his suspense is not ended at the earliest possible instant, the results may be such as I dare not contemplate."

"I know it; that is why I have pushed matters to this point. You will carry that up to her?"

"Yes; and if—"

"No ifs. Lay it before her where she sits and come away. But not beyond call. You are a good woman—I see it in your face—do not watch her as she unfolds this paper. Persons of her temperament do not like to have their emotions observed, and this will cause her emotion. That can not be helped, Miss Porter. Sincerely and honestly I tell you that it is impossible for her best friends to keep her from suffering now; they can only strive to keep that suffering from becoming permanent."

"It is a hard task you have set me," complained the poor woman; "but I will do what I can. Anything must be better for Mrs. Ocumpaugh than the suspense she is now laboring under."

"Remember," I enjoined, with the full force of my secret anxiety, "that no eye but hers must fall upon this drawing. Not that it would convey meaning to anybody but herself, but because it is her affair and her affair only, and you are the woman to respect another person's affairs."

She gave me a final scrutinizing look and left the room.

"God grant that I have made no mistake!" was the inward prayer with which I saw her depart.

My fervency was sincere. I was myself frightened at what I had done.

And what had I done? Sent her a sketch drawn by myself of Doctor Pool and of his office. If it recalled to her, as I felt it must, the remembrance of a certain memorable visit she had once paid there, she would receive me.

When Miss Porter reëntered some fifteen minutes later, I saw that my hazardous attempt had been successful.

"Come," said she; but with no cheerful alacrity, rather with an air of gloom.

"Was—was Mrs. Ocumpaugh very much disturbed by what she saw?"

"I fear so. She was half-asleep when I went in, dreaming as it seemed, and pleasantly. It was cruel to disturb her; indeed I had not the heart, so I just laid the folded paper near her hand and waited, but not too near, not within sight of her face. A few minutes later—interminable minutes to me—I heard the paper rattle, but I did not move. I was where she could see me, so she knew that she was not alone and presently I caught the sound of a strange noise from her lips, then a low cry, then the quick inquiry in sharper and more peremptory tones than I had ever before heard from her, 'Where did this come from? Who has dared to send me this?' I advanced quickly. I told her about you and your desire to see her; how you had asked me to bring her up this little sketch so that she would know that you had real business with her; that I regretted troubling her when she felt so weak, but that you promised revelations or some such thing—at which I thought she grew very pale. Are you quite convinced that you have news of sufficient importance to warrant the expectations you have raised in her?"

"Let me see her," I prayed.

She made a sign and we both left the room.

Mrs. Ocumpaugh awaited me in her own boudoir on the second floor. As we went up the main staircase I was afforded short glimpses of room after room of varying richness and beauty, among them, one so dainty and delicate in its coloring that I presumed to ask if it were that of the missing child.

Miss Porter's look as she shook her head roused my curiosity.

"I should be glad to see her room," I said.

She stopped, seemed to consider the matter for a moment, then advanced quickly and, beckoning me to follow, led me to a certain door which she quietly opened. One look, and my astonishment became apparent. The room before me, while large and sunny, was as simple, I had almost said as bare, as my sister's at home. No luxurious furnishings here, no draperies of silk and damask, no half-lights drawing richness from stained glass, no gleam of silver or sparkle of glass on bedecked dresser or carved mantel. Not even the tinted muslins I had seen in some nurseries; but a plain set of furniture on a plain carpet with but one object of real adornment within the four walls. That was a picture of the Madonna opposite the bed, and that was beautiful. But the frame was of the cheapest—a simple band of oak.

Catching Miss Porter's eye as we quietly withdrew, I ventured to ask whose taste this was.

The answer was short and had a decided ring of disapproval in it.

"Her mother's. Mrs. Ocumpaugh believes in simple surroundings for children."

"Yet she dressed Gwendolen like a princess."

"Yes, for the world's eye. But in her own room she wore gingham aprons which effectually covered up her ribbons and laces."

The motive for all this was in a way evident to me, but somehow what I had just seen did not add to my courage for the coming interview.

We stopped at the remotest door of this long hall. As Miss Porter opened it I summoned up all my nerve, and the next moment found myself standing in the presence of the imposing figure of Mrs. Ocumpaugh drawn up in the embrasure of a large window overlooking the Hudson. It was the same window, doubtless, in which she had stood for two nights and a day watching for some sign from the boats engaged in dragging the river-bed. Her back was to me and she seemed to find it difficult to break away from her fixed attitude; for several minutes elapsed before she turned slowly about and showed me her face.

When she did, I stood appalled. Not a vestige of color was to be seen on cheek, lip or brow. She was the beautiful Mrs. Ocumpaugh still, but the heart which had sent the hues of life to her features, was beating slow — slow — and the effect was heartbreaking to one who had seen her in her prime and the full glory of her beauty as wife and mother.

"Pardon," I faltered out, bowing my head as if before some powerful rebuke, though her lips were silent and her eyes pleading rather than accusing. Truly, I had ventured far in daring to recall to this woman an hour which at this miserable time she probably would give her very life to forget. "Pardon," I repeated, with even a more humble intonation than before, for she did not speak and I hardly knew how to begin the conversation. Still she said nothing, and at last I found myself forced to break the unbearable silence by some definite remark.

"I have presumed," I therefore continued, advancing but a step toward her who made no advance at all, "to send you a hurried sketch of one who says he knows you, that you might be sure I was not one of the many eager but irresponsible men who offer help in your great trouble without understanding your history or that of the little one to whose seemingly unaccountable disappearance all are seeking a clue."

"My history!"

The words seemed forced from her, but no change in eye or look accompanied them; nor could I catch a motion of her lips when she presently added in a far-away tone inexpressibly affecting, "Her history! Did he bid you say that?"

"Doctor Pool? He has given me no commands other than to find the child. I am not here as an agent of his. I am here in Mr. Ocumpaugh's interest and your own; with some knowledge — a little more knowledge than others have perhaps — to aid me in the business of recovering this child. Madam, the police are seeking her in the holes and slums of the great city and at the hands of desperate characters who make a living out of the terrors and griefs of the rich. But this is not where I should look for Gwendolen Ocumpaugh. I should look nearer, just as you have looked nearer; and I should use means which I am sure have not commended themselves to the police. These means you can doubtless put in my hands. A mother knows many things in connection with her child which she neither thinks to impart nor would, under any ordinary circumstances, give up, especially to a stranger. I am not a stranger; you have seen me in Mr. Ocumpaugh's confidence; will you then pardon me if I ask what may strike you as impertinent questions, but which may lead to the discovery of the motive if not to the method of the little one's abduction?"

"I do not understand—" She was trying to shake off her apathy. "I feel confused, sick, almost like one dying. How can I help? Haven't I done everything? I believe that she strayed to the river and was drowned. I still believe her dead. Otherwise we should have news—real news—and we don't, we don't."

The intensity with which she uttered the last two words brought a line of red into her gasping lips. She was becoming human, and for a minute I could not help drawing a comparison between her and her friend Mrs. Carew as the latter had just appeared to me in her little half-denuded house on the other side of the hedge-row. Both beautiful, but owing their charms to quite different sources, I surveyed this woman, white against the pale green of the curtain before which she stood, and imperceptibly but surely the glowing attractions of the gay-hearted widow who had found a child to love, faded before the cold loveliness of this bereaved mother, wan with suffering and alive with terrors of whose depth I could judge from the clutch with which she still held my little sketch.

Meanwhile I had attempted some kind of answer to Mrs. Ocumpaugh's heart-rending appeal.

"We do not hear because she was not taken from you simply for the money her return would bring. Indeed, after hours of action and considerable thinking, I am beginning to doubt if she was taken for money at all. Can you not think of some other motive? Do you not know of some one who wanted the child from—love, let us say?"

"Love?"

Did her lips frame it, or did I see it in her eyes? Certainly I heard no sound, yet I was conscious that she repeated the word in her mind, if not aloud.

"I know I have startled you," I pursued. "But, pardon me—I can not help my presumption—I must be personal—I must even go so far as to probe the wound I have made. You have a claim to Gwendolen not to be doubted, not to be gainsaid. But isn't there some one else who is conscious of possessing certain claims also? I do not allude to Mr. Ocumpaugh."

"You mean—some relative—aunt—cousin—" She was fully human now, and very keenly alert. "Mr. Rathbone, perhaps?"

"No, Mrs. Ocumpaugh, none of these." Then as the paper rattled in her hand and I saw her eyes fall in terror on it, I said as calmly and respectfully as I could: "You have a secret, Mrs. Ocumpaugh; that secret I share."

The paper trembled from her clasp and fell fluttering downward. I pointed at it and waited till our eyes met, possibly that I might give her some encouragement from my look if not from my words.

"I was a boy in Doctor Pool's employ some five years ago, and one day—"

I paused; she had made me a supplicating gesture.

"Shall I not go on?" I finally asked.

"Give me a minute," was her low entreaty. "O God! O God! that I should have thought myself secure all these years, with two in the world knowing my fatal secret!"

"I learned it by accident," I went on, when I saw her eye turn again on mine. "On a certain night six years ago, I was in the office behind an old curtain—you remember the curtain hanging at the left of the doctor's table over that break in the book-shelves. I had no business there. I had been meddling with things which did not belong to me and, when I heard the doctor's step at the door, was glad to shrink into this refuge and wait for an opportunity to escape. It did not come very soon. First he had one patient, then another. The last one was you; I heard your name and caught a glimpse of your face as you went out. It was a very interesting story you told him—I was touched by it though I hardly understood."

"Oh! oh!"

She was swaying from side to side, swaying so heavily that I instinctively pushed forward a chair.

"Sit," I prayed. "You are not strong enough for this excitement."

She glanced at me vaguely, shook her head, but made no move toward accepting the proffered chair. She submitted, however, when I continued to press it upon her; and I felt less a brute and hard-hearted monster when I saw her sitting with folded hands before me.

"I bring this up," said I, "that you may understand what I mean when I say that some one else—another woman, in fact, may feel her claim upon this child greater than yours."

"You mean the real mother. Is she known? The doctor swore—"

"I do not know the real mother. I only know that you are not; that to win some toleration from your mother-in-law, to make sure of your husband's lasting love, you won the doctor over to a deception which secured a seeming heir to the Ocumpaughs. Whose child was given you, is doubtless known to you—"

"No, no."

I stared, aghast.

"What! You do not know?"

"No, I did not wish to. Nor was she ever to know me or my name."

"Then this hope has also failed. I thought that in this mother, we might find the child's abductor."

XVIII-"YOU LOOK AS IF—AS IF—"

I had studiously avoided looking at her while these last few words passed between us, but as the silence which followed this final outburst continued, I felt forced to glance her way if only to see what my next move should be. I found her gazing straight at me with a bright spot on either cheek, looking as if seared there by a red-hot iron.

"You are a detective," she said, as our regards met. "You have known this shameful secret always, yet have met my husband constantly and have never told."

"No, I saw no reason."

"Did you never, when you saw how completely my husband was deceived, how fortunes were bequeathed to Gwendolen, gifts lavished on her, her small self made almost an idol of, because all our friends, all our relatives saw in her a true Ocumpaugh, think it wicked to hold your peace and let this all go on as if she were the actual offspring of my husband and myself?"

"No; I may have wondered at your happiness; I may have thought of the consequences if ever he found out, but—"

I dared not go on; the quick, the agonizing nerve of her grief and suffering had been touched and I myself quailed at the result. Stammering some excuse, I waited for her soundless anguish to subside; then, when I thought she could listen, completed my sentence by saying:

"I did not allow my thoughts to stray quite so far, Mrs. Ocumpaugh. Not till my knowledge of your secret promised to be of use did I let it rise to any proportion in my mind. I had too much sympathy for your difficulties; I have to-day."

This hint of comfort, perhaps from the only source which could afford her any, seemed to move her.

"Do you mean that you are my friend?" she cried. "That you would help me, if any help were possible, to keep my secret and—my husband's love?"

I did not know how to dash the first spark of hope I had seen in her from the beginning of this more than painful interview. To avoid it, I temporized a trifle and answered with ready earnestness:

"I would do much, Mrs. Ocumpaugh, to make the consequences of your act as ineffective as possible and still be true to the interests of Mr. Ocumpaugh. If the child can be found—you wish that? You loved her?"

"O yes, I loved her." There was no mistaking the wistfulness of her tone. "Too well, far too well; only my husband more."

"If you can find her—that is the first thing, isn't it?"

"Yes."

It was a faint rejoinder. I looked at her again.

"You do not wish her found," I suddenly declared.

She started, rose to her feet, then suddenly sat again as if she felt that she could not stand.

"What makes you say that? How dare you? how can you say that? My husband loves her, I love her—she is our own child, if not by birth, by every tie which endears a child to a parent. Has that wicked man—"

"Doctor Pool!" I put in, for she stopped, gasping.

"Yes; Doctor Pool, whom I wish to God I had never seen—has he told you any such lies as that? the man who swore—"

I put out my hand to calm her. I feared for her reason if not for her life.

"Be careful," I enjoined. "Your walls are thick but tones like yours are penetrating." Then as I saw she would be answered, I replied to the question still alive in her face: "No; Doctor Pool has not talked of you. I saw it in your own manner, madam; it or something else. Perhaps it was something else—another secret which I have not shared."

She moistened her lips and, placing her two hands on the knobs of the chair in which she sat, leaned passionately forward. Who could say she was cold now? Who could see anything but a feeling heart in this woman, beautiful beyond all precedent in her passion and her woe?

"It is—it was—a secret. I have to confess to the abnormal. The child did not love me; has never loved me. Lavish as I have been in my affection and caresses, she has never done aught but endure them. Though she believes me her own mother, she has shrunk from me with all the might of her nature from the very first. It was God's punishment for the lie by which I strove to make my husband believe himself the father which in God's providence he was not. I have borne it; but my life has been a living hell. It was that you saw in my face—nothing else."

I was bound to believe her. The child had made her suffer, but she was bent upon recovering her—of course. I dared not contemplate any other alternative. Her love for her husband precluded any other desire on her part. And so I admitted, when after a momentary survey of the task yet before me, I ventured to remark:

"Then we find ourselves once more at the point from which we started. Where shall we look for his child? Mrs. Ocumpaugh, perhaps it would aid us in deciding this question if you told me, sincerely told me, why you had such strong belief in Gwendolen's having been drowned in the river. You did believe this—I saw you at the window. You are not an actress like your friend—you expected to see her body drawn from those waters. For twenty-four hours you expected it, though every one told you it was impossible. Why?"

She crept a step nearer to me, her tones growing low and husky.

"Don't you see? I—I—thought that to escape me, she might have leaped into the water. She was capable of it. Gwendolen had a strong nature. The struggle between duty and repulsion made havoc even in her infantile breast. Besides, we had had a scene that morning—a secret scene in which she showed absolute terror of me. It broke my heart, and when she disappeared in that mysterious way—and—and—one of her shoes was found on the slope, what was I to think but that she had chosen to end her misery—this child! this babe I had loved as my own flesh and blood!—in the river where she had been forbidden to go?"

"Suicide by a child of six! You gave another reason for your persistent belief, at the time, Mrs. Ocumpaugh."

"Was I to give this one?"

"No; no one could expect you to do that, even if there had been no secret to preserve and the child had been your own. But the child did not go to the river. You are convinced of that now, are you not?"

"Yes."

"Where then did she go? Or rather, to what place was she taken? Somewhere near; somewhere within easy reach, for the alarm soon rose and then she could not be found. Mrs. Ocumpaugh, I am going to ask you an apparently trivial and inconsequent question. Was Gwendolen very fond of sweets?"

"Yes."

She was sitting upright now, staring me in the face in unconcealed astonishment and a little fear.

"What sort of candy—pardon me if I seem impertinent—had you in your house on the Wednesday the child disappeared? Any which she could have got at or the nurse given her?"

"There were the confections brought by the caterer; none other that I know of; I did not indulge her much in sweets."

"Was there anything peculiar about these confections either in taste or appearance?"

"I didn't taste them. In appearance they were mostly round and red, with a brandied cherry inside. Why, sir, why do you ask? What have these miserable lumps of sugar to do with Gwendolen?"

"Madam, do you recognize this?"

I took from my pocket the crushed mass of colored sugar and fruit I had picked up from the musty cushions of the old sofa in the walled-up room of the bungalow.

She took it and looked up, staring.

"It is one of them," she cried. "Where did you get it? You look as if—as if—"

"I had come upon a clue to Gwendolen? Madam, I believe I have. This candy has been held in a hot little hand. Miss Graham or one of the girls must have given it to her as she ran through the dining-room or across the side veranda on her way to the bungalow. She did not eat it offhand; she evidently fell asleep before eating it, but she clutched it very tight, only dropping it, I judge, when her muscles were quite relaxed by sleep; and then not far; the folds of her dress caught it, for—"

"What are you telling me?" The interruption was sudden, imperative. "I saw Gwendolen asleep; she held a string in her hand but no candy, and if she did—"

"Did you examine both hands, madam? Think! Great issues hang on a right settlement of this fact. Can you declare that she did not have this candy in one of her little hands?"

"No, I can not declare that."

"Then I shall always believe she did, and this same sweetmeat, this morsel from the table set for your guests on the afternoon of the sixteenth of this month, I found last night in the disused portion of the bungalow walled up by Mr. Ocumpaugh's father, but made accessible since by an opening let into the floor from the cellar. This latter I was enabled to reach by means of a trap-door concealed under the rug in the open part of this same building."

"I—I am all confused. Say that again," she pleaded, starting once more to her feet, but this time without meeting my eyes. "In the disused part of the bungalow? How came you there? No one ever goes there—it is a forbidden place."

"The child has been there—and lately."

"Oh!" her fingers began to tremble and twist themselves together. "You have something more than this to tell me. Gwendolen has been found and—" her looks became uncertain and wandered, as I thought, toward the river.

"She has not been found, but the woman who carried her into that place will soon be discovered."

"How? Why?"

I had risen by this time and could answer her on a level and face to face.

"Because the trail of her steps leads straight along the cellar floor. We have but to measure these footprints."

"And what?—what?"

"We find the abductor."

A silence, during which one long breath issued from her lips.

"Was it a man's or woman's steps?" she finally asked.

"A woman's, daintily shod; a woman of about the size of—"

"Who? Why do you play with my anguish?"

"Because I hate to mention the name of a friend."

"Ah! What do you know of my friends?"

"Not much. I happened to meet one of them, and as she is a very fine woman with exquisitely shod feet, I naturally think of her."

"What do you mean?" Her hand was on my arm, her face close to mine. "Speak! speak! the name!"

"Mrs. Carew."

I had purposely refrained up to this moment from bringing this lady, even by a hint, into the conversation. I did it now under an inner protest. But I had not dared to leave it out. The footprints I alluded to were startlingly like those left by her in other parts of the cellar floor; besides, I felt it my duty to see how Mrs. Ocumpaugh bore this name, notwithstanding my almost completely restored confidence in its owner.

She did not bear it well. She flushed and turned quickly from my side, walking away to the window, where she again took up her stand.

"You would have shown better taste by not following your first impulse," she remarked. "Mrs. Carew's footsteps in that old cellar! You presume, sir, and make me lose confidence in your judgment."

"Not at all. Mrs. Carew's feet have been all over that cellar floor. She accompanied me through it last night, at the time I found this crushed bonbon."

I could see that Mrs. Ocumpaugh was amazed, well-nigh confounded, but her manner altered from that moment.

"Tell me about it."

And I did. I related the doubts I had felt concerning the completeness of the police investigation as regarded the bungalow; my visit there at night with Mrs. Carew, and the discoveries we had made. Then I alluded again to the footprints and the important clue they offered.

"But the child?" she interrupted "Where is the child? If taken there, why wasn't she found there? Don't you see that your conclusions are all wild — incredible? A dream? An impossibility?"

"I go by the signs," I replied. "There seems to be nothing else to go by."

"And you want — you intend, to measure those steps?"

"That is why I am here, Mrs. Ocumpaugh. To request permission to continue this investigation and to ask for the key to the bungalow. Mrs. Carew's is no longer available; or rather, I should prefer to proceed without it."

With sudden impulse she advanced rapidly toward me.

"What is Mrs. Carew doing this morning?" she asked.

"Preparing for departure. She is quite resolved to sail to-day. Do you wish to see her? Do you wish her confirmation of my story? I think she will come, if you send for her."

"There is no need." This after an instant's hesitation. "I have perfect confidence in Mrs. Carew; and in you too," she added, with what she meant for a kind look. She was by nature without coquetry, and this attempt to please, in the midst of an overwhelming distress absorbing all her faculties, struck me as the most pitiful effort I had ever seen. My feeling for her made it very hard for me to proceed.

"Then I may go on?" I said.

"Of course, of course. I don't know where the key is; I shall have to give orders. You will wait a few minutes, somewhere in one of the adjoining rooms, while I look up Mr. Atwater?"

"Certainly."

She was trembling, feverish, impatient.

"ShallInot look up Mr. Atwater for you?" I asked.

"No. I am feeling better. I can go myself."

In another moment she had left the room, having forgotten her own suggestion that I should await her return in some adjoining apartment.

XIX-FRENZY

Five minutes—ten minutes—elapsed and I became greatly impatient. I walked the floor; I stared from the window; I did everything I could think of to pass away these unendurable moments of suspense with creditable self-possession. But I failed utterly.

As the clock ticked off the quarter hour, and then the half, I grew not only impatient but seriously alarmed, and flinging down the book I had taken up as a last resort, stepped from the room, in the hope of coming across some one in the hall whom I could interrogate.

But the house seemed strangely quiet, and when I had walked the full length of the hall without encountering either maid or mistress, I summoned up courage to return to the room I had left and ring the bell.

No answer, though I waited long for it.

Thinking that I had not pressed the button hard enough, I made a second attempt, but again there was no answer.

Was anything amiss? Had she—

My thought did not complete itself. In sudden apprehension of I knew not what, I dashed from the room and made my way down stairs without further ceremony.

The unnatural stillness which had attracted my attention above was repeated on the floor below. No one in the rooms, no one in the passages.

Disturbed as I had not been yet by anything which had occurred in connection with this harrowing affair, I leaped to the nearest door and stepped out on the lawn.

My first glance was toward the river. All was as usual there. With my worst fears dispelled, but still a prey to doubts for which as yet I had no name, I moved toward the kitchen windows, expecting of course to find some one there who would explain the situation to me. But not a head appeared at my call. The kitchen, too, was deserted.

"This is not chance," I involuntarily exclaimed, and was turning toward the stables when I perceived a child, the son of one of the gardeners, crossing the lawn at a run, and hailing him, asked where everybody had gone that the house seemed deserted.

He looked back but kept on running, shouting as he did so:

"I guess they're all down at the bungalow! I'm going there. Men are digging up the cellar. Mrs. Ocumpaugh says she's afraid Miss Gwendolen's body is buried there."

Aghast and perhaps a trifle conscience-stricken, I stood stock-still in the sunshine. So this was what I had done! Driven her to frenzy; roused her imagination to such a point that she saw her darling—always her darling even if another woman's child—lying under the clay across which I had attempted simply to prove that she had been carried. Or—no! I would not think that! A detective of my experience outwitted by this stricken, half-dead woman whom I had trembled to see try to stand upon her feet? Impossible! Yet the thought brought the blood to my cheek.

Digging up the bungalow cellar! That meant destroying those footprints before I had secured a single impression of the same. I should have roused her curiosity only, not her terror.

Now all might be lost unless I could arrive in time to—do what? Order the work stopped? With what face could I do that with her standing by in all the authority of motherhood—frenzied motherhood—seeking the possible body of her child! My affair certainly looked dubious. Yet I started for the bungalow like the rest, and on a run, too. Perhaps Providence would favor me and some expedient suggest itself by which I might still save the clue upon which so many hopes hung.

The excitement which had now drawn every person on the place in the one direction, was at its height as I burst through the thicket into the path running immediately about the bungalow. Those who could get in at the door had done so, filling the room whence Gwendolen had disappeared, with awe-struck men and chattering women. Some had been allowed to descend through the yawning trap-door, down which all were endeavoring to peer, and, fortified by this fact, I armed myself with an appearance of authority despite my sense of presumption, and pushed and worked my own way to these steps, saying that I had come to aid Mrs. Ocumpaugh, whose attention I declared I had been the first to direct to this place.

Struck with my manner if not with my argument, they yielded to my importunity and allowed me to pass down. The stroke of the spade and the harsh voice of the man directing the work greeted my disquieted ears. With a bound I cleared the last half-dozen steps and, alighting on the cellar bottom, was soon able, in spite of the semi-darkness, to look about me and get some notion of the scene.

A dozen men were working — the full corps of gardeners without doubt — and a single glance sufficed to show me that such of the surface as had not been upturned by their spades had been harried by their footsteps. Useless now to promulgate my carefully formed theory, with any hope of proof to substantiate it. The crushed bonbon, the piled-up boxes and the freshly sawed hole were enough without doubt to establish the fact that the child had been carried into the walled-up room above, but the link which would have fixed the identity of the person so carrying her was gone from my chain of evidence for ever. She who should have had the greatest interest in establishing this evidence was leaning on the arm of Miss Porter and directing, with wavering finger and a wild air, the movements of the men, who, in a frenzy caught from her own, dug here and dug there as that inexorable finger pointed.

Sobs choked Miss Porter; but Mrs. Ocumpaugh was beyond all such signs of grief. Her eyes moved; her breast heaved; now and then a confused command left her lips, but that was all. Yet to me she was absolutely terrifying, and it took all the courage left from my disappointment for me to move so as to attract her attention. When I saw that I had succeeded in doing this, I regretted the impulse which had led me to break into her mood. The change which my sudden appearance caused in her was too abrupt; too startling. I feared the effects, and put up my hand in silent deprecation as her lips essayed to move in what might be some very disturbing command. If she heeded it I can not say. What she said was this:

"IT'S THE CHILD—I'M LOOKING FOR THE CHILD!"

"It's the child—I'm looking for the child! She was brought here. You proved that she was brought here. Then why don't we find her, or—or her little innocent body?"

I did not attempt an answer; I dared not—I merely turned away into a corner, where I should be out of the way of the men. A thought was rising in my mind; a thought which might have led to some definite action if her voice had not risen shrilly and with a despairing utterance in these words:

"Useless! It is not here she will be found. I was mad to think it. Pull up your spades and go."

A murmur of relief from one end of the cellar to the other, and every spade was drawn out of the ground.

"I could have told you," ventured one more hardy than the rest, "that there was no use disturbing this old clay for any such purpose. Any one could see that no spade has been at work here before in years."

"I said that I was mad," she repeated, and waved the men away.

Slowly they retreated with clattering spades and a heavy tread. The murmur which greeted them above slowly died out, and the bungalow was deserted by all but our three selves. When quite sure of this, I turned, and Miss Porter's eyes met mine with a reproachful glance easy enough for me to understand.

"I will go, too," whispered Mrs. Ocumpaugh. "Oh! this has been like losing my darling for the second time!"

Real grief is unmistakable. Recognizing the heartfelt tone in which these words were uttered, I recurred to the idea of frenzy with all the sympathy her situation called for. Yet I felt that I could not let her leave before we had come to some understanding. But how express myself? How say here and now in the presence of a sympathetic but unenlightened third party what it would certainly be difficult enough for me to utter to herself in the privacy of that secluded apartment in which we had met and talked before our confidence was broken into by this impetuous act of hers.

Not seeing at the moment any natural way out of my difficulties, I stood in painful confusion, conscious of Miss Porter's eyes and also conscious that unless some miracle came to my assistance I must henceforth play but a sorry figure in this affair, when my eyes, which had fallen to the ground, chanced upon a morsel of paper so insignificant in size and of such doubtful appearance that the two ladies must have wondered to see me stoop and with ill-concealed avidity pick it up and place it in my pocket.

Mrs. Ocumpaugh, whose false strength was fast leaving her, now muttered some words which were quite unintelligible to me, though they caused Miss Porter to make me a motion very expressive of a dismissal. I did not accept it as such, however, without making one effort to regain my advantage. At the foot of the steps I paused and glanced back at Mrs. Ocumpaugh. She was still looking my way, but her chin had fallen on her breast, and she seemed to sustain herself erect only by a powerful effort. Again her pitiable and humiliating position appealed to me, and it was with some indication of feeling that I finally said:

"Am I not to have an opportunity of finishing the conversation so unhappily interrupted, Mrs. Ocumpaugh? I am not satisfied, and I do not believe you can be, with the partial disclosures I then made. Afford me, I pray, a continuation of that interview, if only to make plain to me your wishes. Otherwise I may fall into some mistake—say or do something which I might regret—for matters can not stand where they are. You know that, do you not, madam?"

"Adèle! go! go!" This to Miss Porter. "I must have a few words more with Mr. Trevitt. I had forgotten what I owe him in the frenzy which possessed me."

"Do you wish to talk to himhere?" asked that lady, with very marked anxiety.

"No, no; it is too cold, too dark. I think I can walk to Mrs. Carew's. Will you join me there, Mr. Trevitt?"

I bowed; but as she passed near me in going out, I whispered in her ear:

"I should suggest that we hold our talk anywhere but at Mrs. Carew's house, since she is liable to be the chief subject of our conversation."

"Now?"

"Now, more than ever. Her share in the child's disappearance was not eliminated or affected in any way by the destruction of her footprints."

"I will go back to the house; I will see him in my own room," Mrs. Ocumpaugh suddenly announced to her greatly disturbed companion. "Mr.

Trevitt will follow in a few minutes. I must have time to think—to compose myself—to decide—"

She was evidently thinking aloud. Anxious to save her from any self-betrayal, I hastily interrupted her, saying quietly:

"I will be at your boudoir door in a half-hour from now. I myself have something to think of in the interim."

"Be careful!" It was Miss Porter who stopped to utter this word in my ear. "Be very careful, I entreat. Her heart-strings are strained almost to breaking."

I answered with a look. She could not be more conscious of this than I was.

XX-"WHAT DO YOU KNOW?"

I was glad of that half-hour. I, too, wanted a free moment in which to think and examine the small scrap of paper I had picked up from this cellar floor. In the casual glance I had given it, it had seemed to offer me a fresh clue, quite capable of replacing the old one; and I did not change my mind on a second examination; the shape, the hue, the few words written on it, even the musty smell pervading it, all going to prove it to be the one possible link which could reunite the chain whose continuity I had believed to be gone for ever.

Rejoicing in my good luck, yet conscious of still moving in very troubled waters, I cast a glance in the direction of Mrs. Carew's house, from the door of the bungalow whence I had seen Mrs. Ocumpaugh depart, and asked myself why Mrs. Carew, of all persons in the vicinity, had been the only one to hang back from this scene of excitement. It was not like her to hide herself at such a crisis (how invariably she had followed me in each, and every visit I had paid here!), and though I remembered all her reasons for pre-occupation, her absence under the present conditions bore an aspect of guilt which sent my mind working in a direction which was not entirely new to me, but which I had not as yet resolutely faced.

Guilt! The word recalled that other and similar one uttered by Mr. Rathbone in that adventure which had impressed me as so unreal, and still held its place in my mind as something I had dreamed.

He was looking up when he said it, up the hill, up toward Mrs. Carew's house. He had struck his own breast, but he had looked up, not down; and though I had naturally associated the word he had used with himself—and Miss Graham, with a womanly intuition, had supplied me with an explanation of the same which was neither far-fetched nor unnatural, yet all through this day of startling vicissitudes and unimaginable interviews, faint doubts, bidden and unbidden, had visited my mind, which at this moment culminated in what I might call the irresistible question as to whether he might not have had in mind some one nearer and dearer than himself when he uttered that accusing word.

Her position, as I saw it now, did not make this supposition too monstrous for belief; that is, if she secretly loved this man who did not dare, or was too burdened with responsibility, to woo her. And who can penetrate a woman's mind? To give him—possibly without his knowledge—what every one who knew him declared him to stand in special need of—money and relief from too exacting work—might have seemed motive enough to one of her warm and impulsive temperament, for eliminating the child she cared for, but not as she cared for him. It was hard to think it; it would be harder yet to act upon it; but the longer I stood there brooding, the more I felt my conviction grow that from her and from her alone, we should yet obtain definite traces of the missing child, if only Mrs. Ocumpaugh would uphold me in the attempt.

But would Mrs. Ocumpaugh do this? I own that I had my doubts. Some hidden cause or instinct which I had not been able to reach, though I had plunged deep into the most galling secrets of her life, seemed to stand in the way of her full acceptance of the injury I believed her to have received from Mrs. Carew; or rather, in the way of her public acknowledgment of it. Though she would fain have this upturning of the bungalow cellar pass for an act of frenzy, I could not quite bring myself to look upon it as such since taking a final observation of its condition.

Though her professed purpose had been to seek the body of her child, the spades had not gone deeper than their length. It had been harrowing, not digging, she had ordered, and harrowing meant nothing more than an obliteration of the footprints which I had menaced her with comparing with those of Mrs. Carew. Why this show of consideration to one she might call friend, but who could hold no comparison in her mind with the safety or recovery of the child which, if not hers, was the beloved object of her husband's heart and only too deeply cherished by herself? Did she fear her charming neighbor? Was the bond between them founded on something besides love, and did she apprehend that a discovery of Mrs. Carew's connection with Gwendolen's disappearance would only precipitate her own disgrace and open up to public recognition the false relationship she held toward the little heiress? Hard questions these, but ones which must soon be faced and answered; for wretched as was Mrs. Ocumpaugh's position and truly as I sympathized with her misery, I was none the less resolved to force such acknowledgments from her as would allow me to approach Mrs. Carew with a definite accusation such as even that daring spirit could not withstand.

Thus resolved, and resisting all temptation to hazard an interview with the latter lady before I had seen Mrs. Ocumpaugh again, I made my way up slowly through the grounds and entered by the side door just as my watch told me that the half-hour of my waiting was over.

Miss Porter was in the upper hall, but turned aside at my approach with a meaning gesture in the direction of the boudoir. I thought that her eyes looked red; certainly she was trembling very much; and with this poor preparation for an interview before which the strongest and most experienced man might quail, I advanced for the second time that morning to the door behind which the distracted mother awaited me.

If I knocked I do not remember it. I rather think she opened the door for me herself upon hearing my step in the hall. At all events we were soon standing again face to face, and the battle of our two wills—for it would be nothing less now—had begun.

She was the first to speak. Braving my inquiring look with eyes in whose depths determination struggled with growing despair, she asked me peremptorily, almost wildly:

"Have you told any one? Do you mean to publish my shame to the world? I see decision in your face. Does it mean that? Tell me! Does it mean that?"

"No, madam; far be it from me to harbor such an intention unless driven to it by the greatest necessity. Your secret is your own; my only reason for betraying my knowledge of it was the hope I cherished of its affording us some clue to the identity of Gwendolen's abductor. It has not done so yet, may never do so; then let us leave that topic and return to the clue offered by the carrying of that child into the long-closed room back of the bungalow. Mrs. Ocumpaugh, intentionally or unintentionally, the proof upon which I relied for settling the identity of the person so carrying her has been destroyed."

With a flush which her seemingly bloodless condition made perfectly startling, she drew back, breaking into wild disclaimers:

"I know—I fear—I was too wild—too eager. I thought only of what might lie under that floor."

"In a half-foot of earth, madam? The spades did not enter any deeper."

With a sudden access of courage, born possibly of her despair, she sought neither to attempt denial nor palliate the fact.

"And if this was my intention—though I don't acknowledge it—you must recognize my reason. I do not believe—you can not make me believe—that Gwendolen was carried into that room by Mrs. Carew. But I could see that you believed it, and to save her the shame of such an accusation and all that might follow from it, I—oh, Mr. Trevitt, you do not think this possible! Do you know so little of the impulses of a mind, bewildered as mine has been by intolerable suffering?"

"I can understand madness, and I am willing to think that you were mad just then—especially as no harm has been done and I can still accuse Mrs. Carew of a visit to that room, with the proof in my hand."

"What do you mean?" The steady voice was faltering, but I could not say with what emotion—hope for herself—doubt of me—fear for her friend; it might have been any of these; it might have been all. "Was there a footprint left, then? You say proof. Do you mean proof? A detective does not use that word lightly."

"You may be sure that I would not," I returned. Then in answer to the appeal of her whole attitude and expression: "No, there were no footprints left; but I came upon something else which I have sufficient temerity to believe will answer the same purpose. Remember that my object is first to convince you and afterward Mrs. Carew, that it will be useless for her to deny that she has been in that room. Once that is understood, the rest will come easy; for we know the child was there, and it is not a place she could have found alone."

"The proof!" She had no strength for more than that "The proof! Mr. Trevitt, the proof!"

I put my hand in my pocket, then drew it out again empty, making haste, however, to say:

"Mrs. Ocumpaugh, I do not want to distress you, but I must ask you a few questions first. Do you know the secret of that strangely divided room?"

"Only in a general way. Mr. Ocumpaugh has never told me."

"You have not seen the written account of it?"

"No."

"Nor given into Mrs. Carew's hand such an account?"

"No."

Mrs. Carew's duplicity was assuming definite proportions.

"Yet there is such an account and I have listened to a reading of it."

"You?"

"Yes, madam. Mrs. Carew read it to me last night in her own house. She told me it came to her from your hands. You see she is not always particular in her statements."

A lift of the hand, whether in deprecation or appeal I could not say, was all the answer this received. I saw that I must speak with the utmost directness.

"This account was in the shape of a letter on several sheets of paper. These sheets were very old, and were torn as well as discolored. I had them in my hand and noticed that a piece was lacking from one of them. Mrs. Ocumpaugh, are you ready to repeat that Mrs. Carew did not receive this old letter from you or obtain it in any way you know of from the house we are now in?"

"I had rather not be forced to contradict Mrs. Carew," was the low reply; "but in justice to you I must acknowledge that I hear of this letter for the first time. God grant—but what can any old letter have to do with the agonizing question before us? I am not strong, Mr. Trevitt—I am suffering—do not confuse and burden me, I pray—"

"Pardon, I am not saying one unnecessary word. These old sheets—a secret from the family—did not come from this house. Whence, then, did they come into Mrs. Carew's possession? I see you have forestalled my answer; and if you will now glance at this end of paper, picked up by me in your presence from the cellar floor across which we both know that her footsteps have passed, you will see that it is a proof capable of convicting her of the fact."

I held out the scrap I now took from my pocket.

Mrs. Ocumpaugh's hand refused to take it or her eyes to consult it.

Nevertheless I still held it out.

"Pray read the few words you will find there," I urged. "They are in explanation of the document itself, but they will serve to convince you that the letter to which they were attached, and which is now in Mrs. Carew's hands, came from that decaying room."

"No, no!" The gesture which accompanied this exclamation was more than one of refusal, it was that of repulse. "I can not see—I do not need to—I am convinced."

"Pardon me, but that is not enough, Mrs. Ocumpaugh. I want you to be certain. Let me read these words. The story they prefaced is unknown to you; let it remain so; all I need to tell you about it is this: that it was written by Mr. Ocumpaugh's father—he who raised this partition and who is the undoubted author of these lines. Remember that they headed the letter:

"'Perish with the room whose ceiling oozes blood! If in time to come any man reads these lines, he will know why I pulled down the encircling wall built by my father, and why I raised a new one across this end of the pavilion.'"

Mrs. Ocumpaugh's eyes opened wide in horror.

"Blood!" she repeated. "A ceiling oozing blood!"

"An old superstition, Mrs. Ocumpaugh, quite unworthy your attention at this moment. Do not let your mind dwell upon that portion of what I have read, but on the word 'room.' 'Perish with the room!' We know what room was meant; there can be but one. I have myself seen the desk from which these sheets were undoubtedly taken—and for them to be in the hand of a certain person argues—" Mrs. Ocumpaugh's hand went up in dissuasion, but I relentlessly finished—"that she has been in that room! Are you more than convinced of this now? Are you sure?"

She did not need to make reply; eyes and attitude spoke for her. But it was the look and attitude of despair, not hope. Evidently she had the very greatest reason to fear Mrs. Carew, who possibly had her hard side as well as her charming one.

To ease the situation, I spoke what was in both our minds.

"I see that you are sure. That makes my duty very plain, Mrs. Ocumpaugh. My next visit must be upon Mrs. Carew."

The spirit which, from the beginning of this later interview, had infused fresh strength into her feeble frame, seemed to forsake her at this simple declaration; her whole form drooped, and the eyes, which had rested on mine, turned in their old way to the river.

I took advantage of this circumstance.

"Some one who knows you well, who knows the child well, dropped the wrong shoe into the river."

A murmur, nothing more, from Mrs. Ocumpaugh's set lips.

"Could it—I do not say that it was—I don't see any reason why it should be—but could it have been Mrs. Carew?"

Not a sound this time, not a sound.

"She was down at the dock that night. Did you know it?"

A gesture, but whether of assent or dissent I could not tell.

"We know of no other person who was there but the men employed."

"What do you know?"

With all her restraint gone—a suffering and despairing woman, Mrs. Ocumpaugh was on her knees, grasping my arm with both hands.

"Quit this torture! tell me that you know it all and leave me to—to—die!"

"Madam!"

I was confounded; and as I looked at her face, strained back in wild appeal, I was more than confounded, I was terrified.

"Madam, what does this mean? Are you—you—"

"Lock the door!" she cried; "no one must come in here now. I have said so much that I must say more. Listen and be my friend; oh, be my friend!Those were my footsteps you saw in the bungalow. It was I who carried Gwendolen into that secret hole."

XXI-PROVIDENCE

Had I suspected this? Had all my efforts for the last half-hour been for the purpose of entrapping her into some such avowal? I do not know. My own feelings at the time are a mystery to me; I blundered on, with a blow here and a blow there, till I hit this woman in a vital spot, and achieved the above mentioned result.

I was not happy when I reached it. I felt no elation; scarcely any relief. It all seemed so impossible. She marked the signs of incredulity in my face and spoke up quickly, almost sharply:

"You do not believe me. I will prove the truth of what I say. Wait — wait!" — and running to a closet, she pulled out a drawer — where was her weakness now? — and brought from it a pair of soiled white slippers. "If the house had been ransacked," she proceeded pantingly, "these would have told their own tale. I was shocked when I saw their condition, and kept my guests waiting till I changed them. Oh, they will fit the footprints." Her smile was ghastly. Softly she set the shoes down. "Mrs. Carew helped me; she went for the child at night. Oh, we are in a terrible strait, we two, unless you will stand by us like a friend — and you will do that, won't you, Mr. Trevitt? No one else knows what I have just confessed — not even Doctor Pool, though he suspects me in ways I never dreamed of. Money shall not stand in the way — I have a fortune of my own now — nothing shall stand in the way, if you will have pity on Mrs. Carew and myself and help us to preserve our secret."

"Madam, what secret? I pray you to make me acquainted with the whole matter in all its details before you ask my assistance."

"Then you do not know it?"

"Not altogether, and I must know it altogether. First, what has become of the child?"

"She is safe and happy. You have seen her; you mentioned doing so just now."

"Harry?"

"Harry."

I rose before her in intense excitement. What a plot! I stood aghast at its daring and the success it had so nearly met with.

"I've had moments of suspicion," I admitted, after a short examination of this beautiful woman's face for the marks of strength which her part in this plot seemed to call for. "But they all vanished before Mrs. Carew's seemingly open manner and the perfect boyishness of the child. Is she an actress too—Gwendolen?"

"Not when she plays horse and Indian and other boyish games. She is only acting out her nature. She has no girl tastes; she is all boy, and it was by means of these instincts that Mrs. Carew won her. She promised her that if she would leave home and go with her to Europe she would cut her hair and call her Harry, and dress her so that every one would think her a boy. And she promised her something else—that she should go to her father—Gwendolen idolizes Mr. Ocumpaugh."

"But—"

"I know. You wonder why, if I loved my husband, I should send away the one cherished object of his life. It is because our love was threatened by this very object. I saw nothing but death and chaos before me if I kept her. My husband adores the child, but he hates and despises a falsehood and my secret was threatened by the one man who knows it—your Doctor Pool. My accomplice once, he declared himself ready to become my accuser if the child remained under the Ocumpaugh roof one day after the date he fixed for her removal."

"Ah!" I ejaculated, with sudden comprehension of the full meaning of the scrawls I had seen in so many parts of the grounds. "And by what right did he demand this? What excuse did he give you? His wish for money, immense money—old miser that he is!"

"No; for money I could have given him. His motive is a less tangible one. He has scruples, he says—religious scruples following a change of heart. Oh, he was a cruel man to meet, determined, inexorable. I could not move or influence him. The proffer of money only hurt my cause. A fraud had been perpetrated, he said, and Mr. Ocumpaugh must know it. Would I confess the truth to him myself? No. Then he would do so for me and bring proofs to substantiate his statements. I thought all was lost—my husband's confidence, his love, his pleasure even in the child, for it was his own blood that he loved in her, and her connection with his family of whose prestige he has an exaggerated idea. Made desperate by the thought, I faced this cruel doctor—(it was in his own office; he had presumed upon that old secret linking us together to summon me there)—and told him solemnly that rather than do this I would kill myself. And he almost bade me, 'Kill!' but refrained when the word had half left his lips and changed it to a demand for the child's immediate removal from the benefits it enjoyed under false pretenses."

And from this Mrs. Ocumpaugh went on to relate how he had told her that Gwendolen had inherited fortunes because she was believed to be an Ocumpaugh; that not being an Ocumpaugh she must never handle those fortunes, winding up with some such language as this: "Manage it how you will, only relieve me from the oppression of feeling myself a party to the grossest of deceptions. Can not the child run away and be lost? I am willing to aid you in that, even to paying for her bringing up in some decent, respectable way, such as would probably have been her lot if you had not interfered to place her in the way of millions." It was a mad thought, half meant and apparently wholly impossible to carry out without raising suspicions as damaging as confession itself. But it took an immediate hold upon the miserable woman he addressed, though she gave little evidence of it, for he proceeded to add in a hard tone: "That or immediate confession to your husband, with me by to substantiate your story. No slippery woman's tricks will go down with me. Fix the date here and now and I promise to stand back and await the result in total silence. Dally with it by so much as an hour, and I am at your gates with a story that all must hear." Is it a matter of wonder that the stricken woman, without counsel and prohibited, from the very nature of her secret, from seeking counsel, uttered the first one that came to mind and went home to brood over her position and plan how she could satisfy his demands with the least cost to herself, her husband and the child?

Mr. Ocumpaugh was in Europe. This was her one point of comfort. What was done could be done in his absence, and this fact greatly minimized any risk she was likely to incur. When he returned he would find the house in mourning, for she had already decided within herself that only by apparent death could this child be safely robbed of her endowments as an Ocumpaugh and an heiress. He would grieve, but his grief would lack the sting of shame, and so in course of time would soften into a lovely memory of one who had been as the living sunshine to him and, like the sunshine, brief in its shining. Thus and thus only could she show her consideration for him. For herself no consideration was possible. It must always be her fate to know the child alive yet absolutely removed from her. This was a sorrow capable of no alleviation, for Gwendolen was passionately dear to her, all the dearer, perhaps, because the mother-thirst had never been satisfied; because she had held the cup in hand but had never been allowed to drink. The child's future—how to rob her of all she possessed, yet secure her happiness and the prospect of an honorable estate—ah, there was the difficulty! and one she quite failed to solve till, in a paroxysm of terror and despair, after five sleepless nights, she took Mrs. Carew into her confidence and implored her aid.

The free, resourceful, cheery nature of the broader-minded woman saw through the difficulty at once. "Give her to me," she cried. "I love little children passionately and have always grieved over my childless condition. I will take Gwendolen, raise her and fill her little heart so full of love she will never miss the magnificence she has been brought to look upon as her birthright. Only I shall have to leave this vicinity — perhaps the country."

"And you would be willing?" asked the poor mother — mother by right of many years of service, if not of blood.

The answer broke her heart though it was only a smile. But such a smile — confident, joyous, triumphant; the smile of a woman who has got her heart's wish, while she, she, must henceforth live childless.

So that was settled, but not the necessary ways and means of accomplishment; those came only with time. The two women had always been friends, so their frequent meetings in the green boudoir did not waken a suspicion. A sudden trip to Europe was decided on by Mrs. Carew and by degrees the whole plot perfected. In her eyes it looked feasible enough and they both anticipated complete success. Having decided that the scheme as planned by them could be best carried out in the confusion of a great entertainment, cards were sent out for the sixteenth, the date agreed upon in the doctor's office as the one which should see a complete change in Gwendolen's prospects. It was also settled that on the same day Mrs. Carew should bring home, from a certain small village in Connecticut, her little nephew who had lately been left an orphan. There was no deception about this nephew. Mrs. Carew had for some time supplied his needs and paid for his board in the farm-house where he had been left, and in the emergency which had just come up, she took care to publish to all her friends that she was going to bring him home and take him with her to Europe. Further, a market-man and woman with whom Mrs. Carew had had dealings for years were persuaded to call at her house shortly after three that afternoon, to take this nephew of hers by a circuitous and prolonged ride through the country to an institution in which she had had him entered under an assumed name. All this in one day.

Meanwhile Mrs. Carew undertook to open with her own hands a passage from the cellar of the bungalow into the long closed room behind the partition. This was to insure such a safe retreat for the child during the first search, that by no possibility could anything be found to contradict the testimony of the little shoe which Mrs. Ocumpaugh purposed presenting to all eyes as found on the slope leading to that great burial-place, the river. Otherwise the child might have been passed over to Mrs. Carew at once. All this being decided upon, each waited to perform the part assigned her—Mrs. Carew in a fever of delight—for she was passionately devoted to Gwendolen and experienced nothing but rapture at the prospect of having this charming child all to herself—Mrs. Ocumpaugh, whose only recompense would be freedom from a threatening exposure which would cost her the only thing she prized, her husband's love, in a condition of cold dread, relieved only by the burning sense of the necessity of impressing upon the whole world, and especially upon Mr. Ocumpaugh, an absolute belief in the child's death.

This was her first care. To this her mind clung with an agony of purpose which was the fittest preparation possible for real display of feeling when the time came. But she forgot one thing—they both forgot one thing—that chance or Providence might ordain that witnesses should be on the road below Homewood to prove that the child did not cross the track at the time of her disappearance. To them it seemed enough to plead the child's love for the water, her desire to be allowed to fish, the opportunity given her to escape, and—the little shoes. Such short-sightedness in face of a great peril could be pardoned Mrs. Ocumpaugh on the verge of delirium under her cold exterior, but Mrs. Carew should have taken this possibility into account; and would have done so, probably, had she not been completely absorbed in the part she would be called upon to play when the exchange of children should be made and Gwendolen be intrusted to her charge within a dozen rods of her own home. This she could dwell on with the whole force of her mind; this she could view in all its relations and make such a study of as to provide herself against all contingencies. But the obvious danger of a gang of men being placed just where they could serve as witnesses, in contradiction of the one fact upon which the whole plot was based, never even struck her imagination.

The nursery-governess whose heart was divided between her duty to the child and her strong love of music, was chosen as their unconscious accomplice in this fraud. As the time for the great musicale approached, she was bidden to amuse Gwendolen in the bungalow, with the understanding that if the child fell asleep she might lay her on the divan, and so far leave her as to take her place on the bench outside where the notes of the solo singers could reach her. That Gwendolen would fall asleep and fall asleep soon, the wretched mother well knew, for she had given her a safe but potent sleeping draft which could not fail to insure a twelve hours' undisturbed slumber to so healthy a child. The fact that the little one had shrunk more than ever from her attentions that morning both hurt and encouraged her. Certainly it would make it easier for Mrs. Carew to influence Gwendolen. In her own mind filled with terrible images of her husband's grief and her long prospective dissimulation, one picture rose in brilliant contrast to the dark one embodying her own miserable future and that of the soon-to-be bereaved father. It was that of the perfect joy of the hungry-hearted child in the arms of the woman she loved best. It brought her cheer—it brought her anguish. It was a salve to her conscience and a mortal thrust in an already festering wound. She shut it from her eyes as much as possible,—and so, the hour came.

We know its results—how far the scheme succeeded and whence its great failure arose. Gwendolen fell asleep almost immediately on reaching the bungalow and Miss Graham, dreaming no harm and having the most perfect confidence in Mrs. Ocumpaugh, took advantage of the permission she had received, and slipped outside to sit on the bench and listen to the music. Presently Mrs. Ocumpaugh appeared, saying that she had left her guests for a moment just to take a look at Gwendolen and see if all were well with her.

As she needed no attendance, Miss Graham might stay where she was. And Miss Graham did, taking great pleasure in the music, which was the finest she had ever heard. Meanwhile Mrs. Ocumpaugh entered the bungalow, and, untying the child's shoes as she had frequently done before when she found her asleep, she lifted her and carried her just as she was down the trap, the door of which she had previously raised. The darkness lurking in such places, a darkness which had rendered it so impenetrable at midnight, was relieved to some extent in daylight by means of little grated openings in the wall under the beams, so that her chief difficulty lay in holding up her long dress and sustaining the heavy child at the same time. But the exigency of the moment and her apprehension lest Miss Graham should reënter the bungalow before she could finish her task and escape, gave great precision to her movements, and in an incredibly short space of time she had reached those musty precincts which, if they should not prove the death of the child, would safely shelter her from every one's eye, till the first excitement of her loss was over, and the conviction of her death by drowning became a settled fact in every mind.

Mrs. Ocumpaugh's return was a flight. She had brought one of the little shoes with her, concealed in a pocket she had made especially for it in the trimmings of her elaborate gown. She found the bungalow empty, the trap still raised, and Miss Graham, toward whom she cast a hurried look through the window, yet in her place, listening with enthralled attention to the great tenor upon whose magnificent singing Mrs. Ocumpaugh had relied for the successful carrying out of what she and Mrs. Carew considered the most critical part of the plot. So far then, all was well. She had but to drop the trap-door carefully to its place, replace the corner of the carpet she had pulled up, push down with her foot the two or three nails she had previously loosened, and she would be quite at liberty to quit the place and return to her guests.

But she found that this was not as easy as she had imagined. The clogs of a terrible, almost a criminal, consciousness held back her steps. She stumbled as she left the bungalow and stopped to catch her breath as if the oppression of the room in which she had immured her darling had infected the sunny air of this glorious day and made free breathing an impossibility. The weights on her feet were so palpable to her that she unconsciously looked down at them. This was how she came to notice the dust on her shoes. Alive to the story it told, she burst the spell which held her and made a bound toward the house.

Rushing to her room she shook her skirts and changed her shoes, and thus freed from all connecting links with that secret spot, reëntered among her guests, as beautiful and probably as wretched a woman as the world contained that day.

Yet not as wretched as she could be. There were depths beneath these depths. If he should ever know! If he should ever come to look at her with horrified, even alienated eyes! Ah, that were the end—that would mean the river for her—the river which all were so soon to think had swallowed the little Gwendolen. Was that Miss Graham coming? Was the stir she now heard outside, the first indication of the hue and cry which would soon ring through the whole place and her shrinking heart as well? No, no, not yet. She could still smile, must smile and smite her two glove-covered hands together in simulated applause of notes and tones she did not even hear. And no one noted anything strange in that smile or in that gracious bringing together of hands, which if any one had had the impulse to touch—

But no one thought of doing that. A heart may bleed drop by drop to its death in our full sight without our suspecting it, if the eyes above it still beam with natural brightness. And hers did that. She had always been called impassive. God be thanked that no warmth was expected from her and that no one would suspect the death she was dying, if she did not cry out. But the moment came when she did cry out. Miss Graham entered, told her story, and all Mrs. Ocumpaugh's pent-up agony burst its bounds in a scream which to others seemed but the natural outburst of an alarmed mother. She fled to the bungalow, because that seemed the natural thing to do, and never forgetting what was expected of her, cried aloud in presence of its emptiness: "The river! the river!" and went stumbling down the bank.

The shoe was near her hand and she drew it out as she went on. When they found her she had fainted; the excess of excitement has this natural outcome. She did not have to play a part, the humiliation of her own deed and the terrors yet to come were eating up her very soul. Then came the blow, the unexpected, overwhelming blow of finding that the deception planned with such care—a deception upon the success of which the whole safety of the scheme depended—was likely to fail just for the simple reason that a dozen men could swear that the child had never crossed the track. She was dazed—confounded. Mrs. Carew was not by to counsel her; she had her own part in this business to play; and Mrs. Ocumpaugh, conscious of being mentally unfit for any new planning, conscious indeed of not being able to think at all, simply followed her instinct and held to the old cry in face of proof, of persuasion, of reason even; and so, did the very wisest thing possible, no one expecting reason in a mother reeling under such a vital shock.

But the cooler, more subtile and less guilty Mrs. Carew had some judgment left, if her friend had lost hers. Her own part had been well played. She had brought her nephew home without giving any one, not even the maid she had provided herself with in New York, an opportunity to see his face; and she had passed him over, dressed in quite different clothes, to the couple in the farm-wagon, who had carried him, as she supposed, safely out of reach and any possibility of discovery. You see her calculations failed here also. She did not credit the doctor with even the little conscience he possessed, and, unconscious of his near waiting on the highway in anxious watch for the event concerning which he had his own secret doubts, she deluded herself into thinking that all they had to fear was a continuation of the impression that Gwendolen had not gone down to the river and been drowned.

When, therefore, she had acted out her little part—received the searching party and gone with them all over the house even to the door of the room where she said her little nephew was resting after his journey — (Did they look in? Perhaps, and perhaps not, it mattered little, for the bed had been arranged against this contingency and no one but a detective bent upon ferreting out crime would have found it empty)—she asked herself how she could strengthen the situation and cause the theory advanced by Mrs. Ocumpaugh to be received, notwithstanding the evidence of seeming eye-witnesses. The result was the throwing of a second shoe into the water as soon as it was dark enough for her to do this unseen. As she had to approach the river by her own grounds, and as she was obliged to choose a place sufficiently remote from the lights about the dock not to incur the risk of being detected in her hazardous attempt, the shoe fell at a spot farther down stream than the searchers had yet reached, and the intense excitement I had myself seen in Mrs. Ocumpaugh's face the day I made my first visit to Homewood, sprang from the agony of suspense with which she watched, after twenty-four hours of alternating expectation and disappointment, the finding of this second shoe which, with fanatic confidence, she hoped would bring all the confirmation to be desired of her oft-repeated declaration that the child would yet be found in the river.

Meanwhile, to the infinite dismay of both, the matter had been placed in the hands of the police and word sent to Mr. Ocumpaugh, not that the child was dead, but missing. This meant world-wide publicity and the constant coming and going about Homewood of the very men whose insight and surveillance were most to be dreaded. Mrs. Ocumpaugh sank under the terrors thus accumulating upon her; but Mrs. Carew, of different temperament and history, rose to meet them with a courage which bade fair to carry everything before it.

As midnight approached (the hour agreed upon in their compact) she prepared to go for Gwendolen. Mrs. Ocumpaugh, who had not forgotten what was expected of her at that hour, roused as the clock struck twelve, and uttering a loud cry, rushed from her place in the window down to the lawn, calling out that she had heard the men shout aloud from the boats. Her plan was to draw every one who chanced to be about, down to the river bank, in order to give Mrs. Carew full opportunity to go and come unseen on her dangerous errand. And she apparently succeeded in this, for by the time she had crept back in seeming disappointment to the house, a light could be seen burning behind a pink shade in one of Mrs. Carew's upper windows—the signal agreed upon between them of the presence of Gwendolen in her new home.

But small was the relief as yet. The shoe had not been found, and at any moment some intruder might force his way into Mrs. Carew's house and, in spite of all her precautions, succeed in obtaining a view of the little Harry and recognize in him the missing child.

Of these same precautions some mention must be made. The artful widow had begun by dismissing all her help, giving as an excuse her speedy departure for Europe, and the colored girl she had brought up from New York saw no difference in the child running about the house in its little velvet suit from the one who, with bound-up face and a heavy shade over his eyes, came up in the cars with her in Mrs. Carew's lap. Her duties being limited to a far-off watch on the child to see that it came to no harm, she was the best witness possible in case of police intrusion or neighborhood gossip. As for Gwendolen herself, the novelty of the experience and the prospect held out by a speedy departure to "papa's country" kept her amused and even hilarious. She laughed when her hair was cut short, darkened and parted. She missed but one thing, and that was her pet plaything which she used to carry to bed with her at night. The lack of this caused some tears—a grief which was divined by Mrs. Ocumpaugh, who took pains to assuage it in the manner we all know.

But this was after the finding of the second shoe; the event so long anticipated and so little productive. Somehow, neither Mrs. Carew nor Mrs. Ocumpaugh had taken into consideration the fact of the child's shoes being rights and lefts, and when this attempt to second the first deception was decided on, it was thought a matter of congratulation that Gwendolen had been supplied with two pairs of the same make and that one pair yet remained in her closet. The mate of that shown by Mrs. Ocumpaugh was still on the child's foot in the bungalow, but there being no difference in any of them, what was simpler than to take one of these and fling it where it would be found. Alas! the one seized upon by Mrs. Carew was for the same foot as that already shown and commented on, and thus this second attempt failed even more completely than the first, and people began to cry, "A conspiracy!"

And a conspiracy it was, but one which might yet have succeeded if Doctor Pool's suspicion of Mrs. Ocumpaugh's intentions, and my own secret knowledge of Mrs. Ocumpaugh's real position toward this child, could have been eliminated from the situation. But with those two factors against them, detection had crept upon them in unknown ways, and neither Mrs. Ocumpaugh's frantic clinging to the theory she had so recklessly advanced, nor Mrs. Carew's determined effort to meet suspicion with the brave front calculated to disarm it, was of any avail. The truth would have its way and their secret stood revealed.

This was the story told me by Mrs. Ocumpaugh; not in the continuous and detailed manner I have here set down, but in disjointed sentences and wild bursts of disordered speech. When it was finished she turned upon me eyes full of haggard inquiry.

"Our fate is in your hands," she falteringly declared. "What will you do with it?"

It was the hardest question which had ever been put me. For minutes I contemplated her in a silence which must have been one prolonged agony to her. I did not see my way; I did not see my duty. Then the fifty thousand dollars!

At last, I replied as follows:

"Mrs. Ocumpaugh, if you will let me advise you, as a man intensely interested in the happiness of yourself and husband, I would suggest your meeting him at quarantine and telling him the whole truth."

"I would rather die," said she.

"Yet only by doing what I suggest can you find any peace in life. The consciousness that others know your secret will come between you and any satisfaction you can ever get out of your husband's continued confidence. A wrong has been done; you are the only one to right it."

"I can not. I can die, but I can not do that."

And for a minute I thought she would die then and there.

"Doctor Pool is a fanatic; he will pursue you until he is assured that the child is in good hands."

"You can assure him of that now."

"Next month his exactions may take another direction. You can never trust a man who thinks he has a mission. Pardon my presumption. No mercenary motive prompts what I am saying now."

"So you intend to publish my story, if I do not?"

I hesitated again. Such questions can not be decided in a moment. Then, with a certain consciousness of doing right, I answered earnestly:

"To no one but to Mr. Ocumpaugh do I feel called upon to disclose what really concerns no one but yourself and him."

Her hands rose toward me in a gesture which may have been an expression of gratitude or only one of simple appeal.

"He is not due until Saturday," I added gently.

No answer from the cold lips. I do not think she could have spoken if she had tried.

XXII-ON THE SECOND TERRACE

My first step on leaving Homewood was to seek a public telephone. Calling up Doctor Pool in Yonkers, I assured him that he might rest easy as to the young patient to whose doubtful condition he had called my attention. That she was in good hands and was doing well. That I had seen her and would give him all necessary particulars when I came to interview him later in the day. To his uneasy questions I vouchsafed little reply. I was by no means sure of the advisability of taking him into my full confidence. It was enough for him to know that his demands had been complied with without injury to the child.

Before hanging up the receiver, I put him a question on my own behalf. How was the boy in his charge? The growl he returned me was very non-committal, and afforded me some food for thought as I turned back to Mrs. Carew's cottage, where I now proposed to make a final visit.

I entered from the road. The heavily wooded grounds looked desolate. The copper beeches which are the glory of the place seemed to have lost color since I last saw them above the intervening hedges. Even the house, as it gradually emerged to view through the close shrubbery, wore a different aspect from usual. In another moment I saw why. Every shutter was closed and not a vestige of life was visible above or below. Startled, for I had not expected quite so hasty a departure on her part, I ran about to the side door where I had previously entered and rang fit to wake the dead. Only solitary echoes came from within and I was about to curse the time I had lost in telephoning to Doctor Pool, when I heard a slight sound in the direction of the private path, and, leaping hastily to the opening, caught the glimpse of something or somebody disappearing down the first flight of steps.

Did I run? You may believe I did, at least till I had descended the first terrace; then my steps grew gradually wary and finally ceased; for I could hear voices ahead of me on the second terrace to which I had now come, and these voices came from persons standing still. If I rushed on I should encounter these persons, and this was undesirable. I accordingly paused just short of the top, and so heard what raised the moment into one of tragic importance.

One of the speakers was Mrs. Carew—there was no doubting this—the other was Mr. Rathbone. From no other lips than his could I hope to hear words uttered with such intensity, though he was guarded in his speech, or thought he was, which is not always the same thing.

He was pleading with her, and my heart stood still with the sense of threatening catastrophe as I realized the attitude of the pair. He, as every word showed, was still ignorant of Gwendolen's fate, consequently of the identity of the child who I had every reason to believe was at that very moment fluttering a few steps below in the care of the colored maid, whose voice I could faintly hear; she, with his passion to meet and quell, had this secret to maintain; hearing his wild entreaties with one ear and listening for the possible outbursts of the not-to-be-restrained child with the other; mad to go—to catch her train before discovery overwhelmed her, yet not daring to hasten him, for his mood was a man's mood and not to be denied. I felt sorry for her, and cast about in my mind what aid to give the situation, when the passion of his words seized me, and I forgot her position in the interest I began to feel in his.

"HUSH! THERE IS NO DOUBT ON THAT TOPIC; THE CHILD IS DEAD. LET THAT BE UNDERSTOOD BETWEEN US."

"Valerie, Valerie," he was saying, "this is cruelty. You go with no good cause that I can see—put the sea between us, and yet say no word to make the parting endurable. You understand what I suffer—my hateful thoughts, my dread, which is not so much dread as—Oh, that I should say it! Oh, that I should feel it!—hope; guilty, unpardonable hope. Yet you refuse me the little word, the kindly look, which would alleviate the oppression of my feelings and give me the thought of you to counteract this eternal brooding upon Gwendolen and her possible fate. I want a promise—conditional, O God! but yet a promise; and you simply bid me to have patience; to wait—as if a man could wait who sees his love, his life, his future trembling in the balance against the fate of a little child. If you loved me—"

"Hush!" The feeling in that word was not for him. I felt it at once; it was for her secret, threatened every instant she lingered there by some move, by some word which might escape a thoughtless child. "You do not understand me, Justin. You talk with no comprehension of myself or of the event. Six months from now, if all goes well, you will see that I have been kind, not cruel. I can not say any more; I should not have said so much. Go back, dear friend, and let me take the train with Harry. The sea is not impassable. We shall meet again, and then—" Did she pause to look behind her down those steps—to make some gesture of caution to the uneasy child? "you will forgive me for what seems cruelty to you now. I can not do differently. With all the world weeping over the doubtful fate of this little child, you can not expect me to—to make any promise conditional upon herdeath."

The man's cry drove the irony of the situation out of my mind.

"Puerilities! all puerilities. A man's life—soul—are worth some sacrifices. If you loved me—" A quick ingathering of his breath, then a low moan, then the irrepressible cry she vainly sought to hush, "O Valerie, you are silent! You do not love me! Two years of suffering! two years of repression, then this delirium of hope, of possibility, and yousilent! I will trouble you no more. Gwendolen alive or Gwendolen dead, what is it to me! I—"

"Hush! there is no doubt on that topic; the child isdead. Let that be understood between us." This was whispered, and whispered very low, but the air seemed breathless at that moment and I heard her. "This is my last word to you. You will have your fortune, whether you have my love or not. Remember that, and—"

"Auntie, make Dinah move away; I want to see the man you are talking to."

Gwendolen had spoken.

XXIII-A CORAL BEAD

"What's that?"

It was Mr. Rathbone who first found voice.

"To what a state have I come when in every woman's face, even in hers who is dearest, I see expressions I no longer understand, and in every child's voice catch the sound of Gwendolen's?"

"Harry's voice is not like Gwendolen's," came in desperate protest from the ready widow. A daring assertion for her to make to him who had often held this child in his arms for hours together. "You are not yourself, Justin. I am sorry. I—I—" Almost she gave her promise, almost she risked her future, possibly his, by saying, under the stress of her fears, what her heart did not prompt her to, when—

A quick move on her part, a low cry on his, and he came rushing up the steps.

I had advanced at her hesitating words and shown myself.

When Mr. Rathbone was well up the terrace (he hardly honored me with a look as he went by), I slowly began my descent to where she stood with her back toward me and her arms thrown round the child she had evidently called to her in her anxiety to conceal the little beaming face from this new intruder.

That she had not looked as high as my face I felt assured; that she would not show me hers unless I forced her to seemed equally certain. Every step I took downward was consequently of moment to me. I wondered how I should come out of this; what she would do; what I myself should say. The bold course commended itself to me. No more circumlocution; no more doubtful playing of the game with this woman. I would take the bull by the horns and—

I had reached the step on which she crouched. I could catch sight of the child's eyes over her shoulder, a shoulder that quivered—was it with the storm of the last interview, or with her fear of this? I would see.

Pausing, I said to her with every appearance of respect, but in my most matter-of-fact tones:

"Mrs. Carew, may I request you to send Gwendolen down to the girl I see below there? I have something to say to you before you leave."

Gwendolen!

With a start which showed how completely she was taken by surprise, Mrs. Carew rose. She may have recognized my voice and she may not; it is hard to decide in such an actress. Whether she did or not, she turned with a frown, which gave way to a ravishing smile as her eyes met my face.

"You?" she said, and without any betrayal in voice or gesture that she recognized that her hopes, and those of the friend to whose safety she had already sacrificed so much, had just received their death-blow, she gave a quick order to the girl who, taking the child by the hand, sat down on the steps Mrs. Carew now quitted and laid herself out to be amusing.

Gravely Mrs. Carew confronted me on the terrace below.

"Explain," said she.

"I have just come from Mrs. Ocumpaugh," I replied.

The veiled head dropped a trifle.

"She could not sustain herself! So all is lost?"

"That depends. But I must request you not to leave the country till Mr. Ocumpaugh returns."

The flash of her eye startled me. "Who can detain me," she cried, "if I wish to go?"

I did not answer in kind. I had no wish to rouse this woman's opposition.

"I do not think you will want to go when you remember Mrs. Ocumpaugh's condition. Would you leave her to bear the full burden of this deception alone? She is a broken woman. Her full story is known to me. I have the profoundest sympathy for her. She has only three days in which to decide upon her course. I have advised her to tell the whole truth to her husband."

"You!"

The word was but a breath, but I heard it. Yet I felt no resentment against this woman. No one could, under the spell of so much spirit and grace.

"Did I not advise her right?"

"Perhaps, but you must not detainme. You must do nothing to separate me from this child. I will not bear it. I have experienced for days now what motherhood might be, and nothing on earth shall rob me of my present rights in this child." Then as she met my unmoved countenance: "If you know Mrs.

Ocumpaugh's whole history, you know that neither she nor her husband has any real claim on the child."

"In that you are mistaken," I quickly protested. "Six years of care and affection such as they have bestowed on Gwendolen, to say nothing of the substantial form which these have taken from the first, constitute a claim which all the world must recognize, if you do not. Think of Mr. Ocumpaugh's belief in her relation to him! Think of the shock which awaits him, when he learns that she is not of his blood and lineage!"

"I know, I know." Her fingers worked nervously; the woman was showing through the actress. "But I will not give up the child. Ask anything but that."

"Madam, I have had the honor so far to make but one requirement — that you do not carry the child out of the country — yet."

As I uttered this ultimatum, some influence, acting equally upon both, caused us to turn in the direction of the river; possibly an apprehension lest some word of this conversation might be overheard by the child or the nurse. A surprise awaited us which effectually prevented Mrs. Carew's reply. In the corner of the Ocumpaugh grounds stood a man staring with all his eyes at the so-called little Harry. An expression of doubt was on his face. I knew the minute to be critical and was determined to make the most of it.

"Do you know that man?" I whispered to Mrs. Carew.

The answer was brief but suggestive of alarm.

"Yes, one of the gardeners over there — one of whom Gwendolen is especially fond."

"She's the one to fear, then. Engage his attention while I divert hers."

All this in a whisper while the man was summoning up courage to speak.

"A pretty child," he stammered, as Mrs. Carew advanced toward him smiling. "Is that your little nephew I've heard them tell about? Seems to me he looks like our own little lost one; only darker and sturdier."

"Much sturdier," I heard her say as I made haste to accost the child.

"Harry," I cried, recalling my old address when I was in training for a gentleman; "your aunt is in a hurry. The cars are coming; don't you hear the whistle? Will you trust yourself to me? Let me carry you — I mean pick-a-back, while we run for the train."

The sweet eyes looked up—it was fortunate for Mrs. Carew that no one but myself had ever got near enough to see those eyes or she could hardly have kept her secret—and at first slowly, then with instinctive trust, the little arms rose and I caught her to my breast, taking care as I did so to turn her quite away from the man whom Mrs. Carew was about leaving.

"Come!" I shouted back, "we shall be late!"—and made a dash for the gate.

Mrs. Carew joined me, and none of us said anything till we reached the station platform. Then as I set the child down, I gave her one look. She was beaming with gratitude.

"That saved us, together with the few words I could edge in between his loud regrets at my going and his exclamations of grief over Gwendolen's loss. On the train I shall fear nothing. If you will lift him up I will wrap him in this shawl as if he were ill. Once in New York—are you not going to permit me?"

"To go to New York, yes; but not to the steamer."

She showed anger, but also an admirable self-control. Far off we could catch the sounding thrill of the approaching train.

"I yield," she announced suddenly. And opening the bag at her side, she fumbled in it for a card which she presently put in my hand. "I was going there for lunch," she explained. "Now I will take a room and remain until I hear from you." Here she gave me a quick look. "You do not appear satisfied."

"Yes, yes," I stammered, as I looked at the card and saw her name over that of an inconspicuous hotel in the down-town portion of New York City. "I merely—"

The nearing of the train gave me the opportunity of cutting short the sentence I should have found it difficult to finish.

"Here is the child," I exclaimed, lifting the little one, whom she immediately enveloped in the light but ample wrap she had chosen as a disguise.

"Good-by—Harry."

"Good-by! I like you. Your arms are strong and you don't shake me when you run."

Mrs. Carew smiled. There was deep emotion in her face. "Au revoir!" she murmured in a tone implying promise. Happily I understood the French phrase.

I bowed and drew back. Was I wrong in letting her slip from my surveillance? The agitation I probably showed must have caused her some thought. But she would have been more than a diviner of mysteries to have understood its cause. Her bag, when she had opened it before my eyes, had revealed among its contents a string of remarkable corals. A bead similar in shape, color and marking rested at that very moment over my own heart. Was that necklace one bead short? With a start of conviction I began to believe so and that I was the man who could complete it. If that was so—why, then—then—

It isn't often that a detective's brain reels—but mine did then.

The train began to move—

This discovery, the greatest of all, if I were right, would—

I had no more time to think.

Instinctively, with a quick jump, I made my place good on the rear car.

XXIV-"SHALL I GIVE HIM MY WORD, HARRY?"

I did not go all the way to New York on the train which Mrs. Carew and the child had taken. I went only as far as Yonkers.

When I reached Doctor Pool's house, I thought it entirely empty. Even the office seemed closed. But appearances here could not always be trusted, and I rang the bell with a vigor which must have awakened echoes in the uninhabited upper stories. I know that it brought the doctor to the door, and in a state of doubtful amiability. But when he saw who awaited him, his appearance changed and he welcomed me in with a smile or what was as nearly like one as his austere nature would permit.

"How now! Want your money? Seems to me you have earned it with unexpected ease."

"Not such great ease," I replied, as he carefully closed the door and locked it. "I know that I feel as tired as I ever did in my life. The child is in New York under the guardianship of a woman who is really fond of her. You can dismiss all care concerning her."

"I see—and who is the woman? Name her."

"You do not trust me, I see."

"I trust no one in business matters."

"This is not a business matter—yet."

"What do you mean?"

"I have not asked for money. I am not going to till I can perfectly satisfy you that all deception is at an end so far as Mr. Ocumpaugh at least is concerned."

"Oh, you would play fair, I see."

I was too interested in noting how each of his hands involuntarily closed on itself, in his relief at not being called upon to part with some of his hoardings, to answer with aught but a nod.

"You have your reasons for keeping close, of course," he growled as he led the way toward the basement stairs. "You're not out of the woods, is that it? Or has the great lady bargained with you?—Um? Um?"

He threw the latter ejaculations back over his shoulder as he descended to the office. They displeased me, and I made no attempt to reply. In fact, I had no reply ready. Had I bargained with Mrs. Ocumpaugh? Hardly. Yet—

"She is handsome enough," the old man broke in sharply, cutting in two my self-communings. "You're a fellow of some stamina, if you have got at her secret without making her a promise. So the child is well! That's good! There's one long black mark eliminated from my account. But I have not closed the book, and I am not going to, till my conscience has nothing more to regret. It is not enough that the child is handed over to a different life; the fortunes that have been bequeathed her must be given to him who would have inherited them had this child not been taken for a veritable Ocumpaugh."

"That raises a nice point," I said.

"But one that will drag all false things to light."

"Your action in the matter along with the rest," I suggested.

"True! but do you think I shall stop because of that?"

He did not look as if he would stop because of anything.

"Do you not think Mrs. Ocumpaugh worthy some pity? Her future is a ghastly one, whichever way you look at it."

"She sinned," was his uncompromising reply. "The wages of sin is death."

"But such death!" I protested; "death of the heart, which is the worst death of all."

He shrugged his shoulders, leading the way into the office.

"Let her beware!" he went on surlily. "Last month I saw my duty no further than the exaction of this child's dismissal from the home whose benefits she enjoyed under a false name. To-day I am led further by the inexorable guide which prompts the anxious soul. All that was wrong must be made good. Mr. Ocumpaugh must know on whom his affections have been lavished. I will not yield. The woman has done wrong; and she shall suffer for it till she rises, a redeemed soul, into a state of mind that prefers humiliation to a continuance in a life of deception. You may tell her what I say—that is, if you enjoy the right of conversation with her."

The look he shot me at this was keen as hate and spite could make it. I was glad that we were by this time in the office, and that I could avoid his eye by a quick look about the well-remembered place. This proof of the vindictive pursuit he had marked out for himself was no surprise to me. I expected no less, yet it opened up difficulties which made my way, as well as hers, look dreary in the prospect. He perceived my despondency and smiled; then suddenly changed his tone.

"You do not ask after the little patient I have here. Come, Harry, come; here is some one I will let you see."

The door of my old room swung open and I do not know which surprised me most, the kindness in the rugged old voice I had never before heard lifted in tenderness, or the look of confidence and joy on the face of the little boy who now came running in. So inexorable to a remorseful and suffering woman, and so full of consideration for a stranger's child!

"Almost well," pronounced the doctor, and lifted him on his knee. "Do you know this child's parentage and condition?" he sharply inquired, with a quick look toward me.

I saw no reason for not telling the truth.

"He is an orphan, and was destined for an institution."

"You know this?"

"Positively."

"Then I shall keep the child. Harry, will you stay with me?"

To my amazement, the little arms crept round his neck. A smile grim enough, in my estimation, but not at all frightful to the child, responded to this appeal.

"I did not like the old man and woman," he said.

Doctor Pool's whole manner showed triumph. "I shall treat him better than I did you," he remarked. "I am a regenerate man now."

I bowed; I was very uneasy; there was a question I wanted to ask and could not in the presence of this child.

"He is hardly of an age to take my place," I observed, still under the spell of my surprise, for the child was handling the old man's long beard, and seeming almost as happy as Gwendolen did in Mrs. Carew's arms.

"He will have one of his own," was the doctor's unexpected reply.

I rose. I saw that he did not intend to dismiss the child.

"I should like your word, in return for the relief I have undoubtedly brought you, that you will not molest certain parties till the three days are up which I have mentioned as the limit of my own silence."

"Shall I give him my word, Harry?"

The child, startled by the abrupt address, drew his fingers from the long beard he was playfully stroking and, eyeing me with elfish gravity, seemed to ponder the question as if some comprehension of its importance had found entrance into his small brain. Annoyed at the doctor's whim, yet trusting to the child's intuition, I waited with inner anxiety for what those small lips would say, and felt an infinite relief, even if I did not show it, when he finally uttered a faint "Yes," and hid his face again on the doctor's breast.

My last remembrance of them both was the picture they made as the doctor closed the door upon me, with the sweet, confiding child still clasped in his arms.

XXV-THE WORK OF AN INSTANT

I did not take the car at the corner. I was sure that Jupp was somewhere around, and I had a new mission for him of more importance than any he could find here now. I was just looking about for him when I heard cries and screams at my back, and, turning, saw several persons all running one way. As that way was the one by which I had just come, I commenced running too, and in another moment was one of a crowd collected before the doctor's door. I mean the great front door which, to my astonishment, I had already seen was wide open. The sight which there met my eyes almost paralyzed me.

Stretched on the pavement, spotted with blood, lay the two figures I had seen within the last five minutes beaming with life and energy. The old man was dead, the child dying, one little hand outstretched as if in search of the sympathetic touch which had made the last few hours perhaps the sweetest of his life. How had it happened? Was it suicide on the doctor's part or just pure accident? Either way it was horrible, but—I looked about me; there was a man ready to give explanations. He had seen it all. The doctor had been racing with the child in the long hall. He had opened the door, probably for air. A sudden dash of the child had brought him to the verge, the doctor had plunged to save him, and losing his balance toppled headlong to the street, carrying the child with him.

It was all the work of an instant.

One moment two vigorous figures—the next, a mass of crushed humanity!

A sight to stagger a man's soul! But the thought which came with it staggered me still more.

The force which had been driving Mrs. Ocumpaugh to her fate was removed. Henceforth her secret was safe if—if I chose to have it so.

XXVI-"HE WILL NEVER FORGIVE"

I was walking away when a man touched me. Some one had seen me come from the doctor's office a few minutes before. Of course this meant detention till the coroner should arrive. I quarreled with the circumstances but felt forced to submit. Happily Jupp now came to the front and I was able to send him to New York to keep that watch over Mrs. Carew, without which I could not have rested quiet an hour. One great element of danger was removed most remarkably, if not providentially, from the path I had marked out for myself; but there still remained that of this woman's possible impulses under her great determination to keep Gwendolen in her own care. But with Jupp to watch the dock, and a man in plain clothes at the door of the small hotel she was at present bound for, I thought I might remain in Yonkers contentedly the whole day.

It was not, however, till late the next afternoon that I found myself again in Homewood. I had heard from Jupp. The steamer had sailed, but without two passengers who had been booked for the voyage. Mrs. Carew and the child were still at the address she had given me. All looked well in that direction; but what was the aspect of affairs in Homewood? I trembled in some anticipation of what these many hours of bitter thought might have effected in Mrs. Ocumpaugh. Evidently nothing to lessen the gloom into which the whole household had now fallen. Miss Porter, who came in haste to greet me, wore the careworn look of a long and unrelieved vigil. I was not astonished when she told me that she had not slept a wink.

"How could I," she asked, "when Mrs. Ocumpaugh did not close her eyes? She did not even lie down, but sat all night in an arm-chair which she had wheeled into Gwendolen's room, staring like one who sees nothing out into the night through the window which overlooks the river. This morning we can not make her speak. Her eyes are dry with fever; only now and then she utters a little moan. The doctor says she will not live to see her husband, unless something comes to rouse her. But the papers give no news, and all the attempts of the police end in nothing. You saw what a dismal failure their last attempt was. The child on which they counted proved to be both red-haired and pock-marked. Gwendolen appears to be lost, lost."

In spite of the despair thus expressed my way seemed to open a little.

"I think I can break Mrs. Ocumpaugh's dangerous apathy if you will let me see her again. Will you let me try?"

"The nurse—we have a nurse now—will not consent, I fear."

"Then telephone to the doctor. Tell him I am the only man who can do anything for Mrs. Ocumpaugh. This will not be an exaggeration."

"Wait! I will get his order. I do not know why I have so much confidence in you."

In another fifteen minutes she came to lead me to Mrs. Ocumpaugh.

I entered without knocking; they told me to. She was seated, as they said, in a large chair, but with no ease to herself; for she was not even leaning against its back, but sat with body strained forward and eyes fixed on the ripple of the great river where, from what she had intimated to me in our last interview, she probably saw her grave. There was a miniature in her hand, but I saw at first glance that it was not the face of Gwendolen over which her fingers closed so spasmodically. It was her husband's portrait which she held, and it was his face, aroused and full of denunciation, which she evidently saw in her fancy as I drew nearer her in my efforts to attract her attention; for a shiver suddenly contracted her lovely features and she threw her arms out as if to ward from herself something which she had no power to meet. In doing this her head turned slightly and she saw me.

Instantly the spell under which she sat frozen yielded to a recognition of something besides her own terrible brooding. She let her arms drop, and the lips which had not spoken that morning moved slightly. I waited respectfully. I saw that in another moment she would speak.

"You have come," she panted out at last, "to hear my decision. It is too soon. The steamer has twenty-four hours yet before it can make port. I have not finished weighing my life against the good opinion of him I live for." Then faintly—"Mrs. Carew has gone."

"To New York," I finished.

"No farther than that?" she asked anxiously. "She has not sailed?"

"I did not see how it was compatible with my duty to let her."

Mrs. Ocumpaugh's whole form collapsed; the dangerous apathy was creeping over her again. "You are deciding for me,"—she spoke very faintly—"you and Doctor Pool."

Should I tell her that Doctor Pool was dead? No, not yet. I wanted her to choose the noble course for Mr. Ocumpaugh's sake—yes, and for her own.

"No," I ventured to rejoin. "You are the only one who can settle your own fate. The word must come from you. I am only trying to make it possible for you to meet your husband without any additional wrong to blunt his possible forgiveness."

"Oh, he will never forgive—and I have lost all."

And the set look returned in its full force.

I made my final attempt.

"Mrs. Ocumpaugh, we may never have another moment together in confidence. There is one thing I have never told you, something which I think you ought to know, as it may affect your whole future course. It concerns Gwendolen's real mother. You say you do not know her."

"No, no; do not bring up that. I do not want to know her. My darling is happy with Mrs. Carew—too happy. O God! Give me no opportunity for disturbing that contentment. Don't you see that I am consumed with jealousy? That I might—"

She was roused enough now, cheek and lip and brow were red; even her eyes looked blood-shot. Alarmed, I put out my hand in a soothing gesture, and when her voice stopped and her words trailed off into an inarticulate murmur I made haste to say:

"Listen to my little story. It will not add to your pain, rather alleviate it. When I hid behind the curtain on that day we all regret, I did not slip from my post at your departure. I knew that another patient awaited the doctor's convenience in my own small room, where he had hastily seated her when your carriage drove up. I also knew that this patient had overheard what you said as well as I, for impervious as the door looked I had often heard the doctor's mutterings when he thought I was safe beyond ear-shot, if not asleep. And I wanted to see how she would act when she rejoined the doctor; for I had heard a little of what she had said before, and was quite aware that she could help you out of your difficulty if she wished. She was a married woman, or rather had been, but she had no use for a child, being very poor and anxious to earn her own living. Would she embrace this opportunity to part with it when it came? You may imagine my interest, boy though I was."

"And did she? Was she—"

"Yes. She was ready to make her compact with the doctor just as you had done. Before she left everything was arranged for. It was her child you took—reared—loved—and have now lost."

At another time she might have resented these words, especially the last; but I had roused her curiosity, her panting eager curiosity, and she let them pass altogether unchallenged.

"Did you see this woman? Was she of common blood, common manners? It does not seem possible—Gwendolen is by nature so dainty in all her ways."

"The woman was a lady. I did not see her face, it was heavily veiled, but I heard her voice; it was a lady's voice and—"

"What?"

"She wore beautiful jewels."

"Jewels? You said she was poor."

"So she declared herself, but she had on her neck under her coat a string of beads which were both valuable and of exquisite workmanship. I know, because it broke just as she was leaving, and the beads fell all over the floor, and one rolled my way and I picked it up, scamp that I was, when both their backs were turned in their search for the others."

"A bead—a costly bead—and you were not found out?"

"No, Mrs. Ocumpaugh, she never seemed to miss it. She was too excited over what she had just done to count correctly. She thought she had them all. But this has been in my pocket for six years. Perhaps you have seen its like; I never have, in jeweler's shop or elsewhere, till yesterday."

"Yesterday?" Her great eyes, haggard with suffering, rose to mine, then they fell on the bead which I had taken from my pocket. The cry she gave was not loud, but it effectually settled all my doubts.

"What did you know of Mrs. Carew before she came to — —?" I asked impressively.

For minutes she did not answer; she was trembling like a leaf.

"Her mother!" she exclaimed at last. "Her mother! her own mother! And she never hinted it to me by word or look. Oh, Valerie, Valerie, what tortures we have both suffered! and now you are happy while I—"

Grief seemed to engulf her. Feeling my position keenly, I walked to the window, but soon turned and came back in response to her cry: "I must see Mrs. Carew instantly. Give my orders. I will start at once to New York. They will think I have gone to be on hand to meet Mr. Ocumpaugh, and will say that I have not the strength. Override their objections. I put my whole cause in your hands. You will go with me?"

"With pleasure, madam."

And thus was that terrifying apathy broken up, to be succeeded by a spell of equally terrifying energy.

XXVII-THE FINAL STRUGGLE

She, however, did not get off that night. I dared not push the matter to the point of awakening suspicion, and when the doctor said that the ship was not due for twenty hours and that it would be madness for her to start without a night's rest and two or three good meals, I succumbed and she also to the few hours' delay. More than that, she consented to retire, and when I joined her in her carriage the following morning, it was to find her physically stronger, even if the mind was still a prey to deepest anguish and a torturing indecision. Her nurse accompanied us and the maid called Celia, so conversation was impossible—a fact I did not know whether to be thankful for or not. On the cars she was shielded as much as possible from every one's gaze, and when we reached New York we were driven at once to the Plaza. As I noticed the respect and intense sympathy with which her presence was met by those who saw nothing in her broken aspect but a mother's immeasurable grief, I wondered at the secrets which lie deep down in the hearts of humanity, and what the effect would be if I should suddenly shout aloud:

"She is more wretched than you think. Her suspense is one that the child's return would not appease. Dig deeper into mortal fear and woe if you would know what has changed this beautiful woman into a shadow in five days."

And I myself did not know her mind. I could neither foresee what she contemplated nor what the effect of seeing the child again would have upon her. I only knew that she must never for a moment be out of sight of some one who loved her. I myself never left the hall upon which her room opened, a precaution for which I felt grateful when, late in the evening, she opened the door and, seeing me, stepped out fully dressed for the street.

"Come and tell Sister Angelina that I may be trusted with you," she said. Sister Angelina was the nurse.

Of course I did as she bade me, and after some few more difficulties I succeeded in getting her into a carriage without attracting any special attention. Once there she breathed more easily, and so did I.

"Now take me toher," she said. Whether she meant Mrs. Carew or Gwendolen, I never knew.

I now saw that the hour had come for telling her that she no longer need have any fear of Doctor Pool. Whatever she contemplated must be done with a true knowledge of where she stood and to just what extent her secret remained endangered. I do not know if she felt grateful. I almost think that for the first few minutes she felt rather frightened than relieved to find herself free to act as her wishes and the preservation of her place in her husband's heart and the world's regard impelled her. For she never for a moment seemed to doubt that now the doctor was gone. I would yield to her misery and prove myself the friend she had begged me to be from the first. She turned herself toward me and sought to read my face, but it was rather to find out what I expected of her than what she had yet to fear from me. I noted this and muttered some words of confidence; but her mood had already changed, and they fell on deaf ears.

I was not present at the meeting of the two women. That is, I remained in what they would call a private parlor, while Mrs. Ocumpaugh passed into the inner room, where she knew she would find Mrs. Carew and the child. Nor did I hear much. Some words came through the partition. I caught most of Mrs. Carew's explanation of how she came to give up her new-born child. She was an actress at the time with a London success to her credit, but with no hold as yet in this country. She was booked for a tour the coming season; the husband who might have seen to the child was dead; she had no friends, no relatives here save a brother poorer than herself, and the mother instinct had not awakened. She bartered her child away as she would have parted with any other encumbrance likely to interfere with her career. But—here her voice rose and I heard distinctly: "A fortune was suddenly left me. An old admirer dying abroad bequeathed me two million dollars, and I found myself rich, admired and independent, with no one on earth to care for or to share the happiness of what seemed to me, after the brilliant life I had hitherto led, a dreary inaction. Love had no interest for me. I had had a husband, and that part of my nature had been satisfied. What I wanted now—and the wish presently grew into a passion—was my child. From passion it grew to mania. Knowing the name of her to whom I had yielded it (I had overheard it in the doctor's office), I hunted up your residence and came one day to Homewood.

"Perhaps some old servant can be found there to-day who could tell you of the strange, deeply veiled lady who was found one evening at sunset, clinging to the gate with both hands and sobbing as she looked in at the triumphant little heiress racing up and down the walks with the great mastiff, Don. They will say that it was some poor crazy woman, or some mother who had buried her own little darling; but it was I, Marion, it was I, looking upon the child I had sold for a half-year's independence; I who was broken-hearted now for her smiles and touches and saw them all given to strangers, who had made her a princess, but who could never give her such love as I felt for her then in my madness. I went away that time, but I came again soon with the titles of the adjoining property in my pocket. I could not keep away from the sight of her, and felt that the torture would be less to see her in your arms than not to see her at all."

The answer was not audible, but I could well imagine what it was. As every one knew, the false mother had not long held out against the attractions of the true one. Instinct had drawn the little one to the heart that beat responsive to its own.

What followed I could best judge from the frightened cry which the child suddenly gave. She had evidently waked to find both women at her bedside. Mrs. Carew's "Hush! hush!" did not answer this time; the child was in a frenzy, and evidently turned from one to the other, sobbing out alternately, "I will not be a girl again. I like my horse and going to papa and sailing on the big ocean, in trousers and a little cap," and the softer phrases she evidently felt better suited to Mrs. Ocumpaugh's deep distress: "Don't feel bad, mamma, you shall come see me some time. Papa will send for you. I am going to him." Then silence, then such a struggle of woman-heart with woman-heart as I hope never to be witness to again. Mrs. Ocumpaugh was pleading with Mrs. Carew, not for the child, but for her life. Mr. Ocumpaugh would be in port the next morning; if she could show him the child all would be well. Mr. Trevitt would manage the details; take the credit of having found Gwendolen somewhere in this great city, and that would insure him the reward and them his silence. (I heard this.) There was no one else to fear. Doctor Pool, the cause of all this misery, was dead; and in the future, her heart being set to rest about her secret, she would be happier and make the child happier, and they could enjoy her between them, and she would be unselfish and let Gwendolen spend an hour or more every day with Mrs. Carew, on some such plea as lessons in vocal-training and music.

Thus pleaded Mrs. Ocumpaugh.

But the mother hardly listened. She had eaten with the child, slept with the child and almost breathed with the child for three days now, and the ecstasy of the experience had blinded her to any other claim than her own. She pitied Mrs. Ocumpaugh, pitied most of all her deceived husband, but no grief of theirs could equal that of Rachel crying for her child. Let Mrs. Ocumpaugh remember that when the evil days come. She had separated child from mother! child from mother! Oh, how the wail swept through those two rooms!

I dared not prophesy to myself at this point how this would end. I simply waited.

Their voices had sunk after each passionate outbreak, and I was only able to catch now and then a word which told me that the struggle was yet going on.

But finally there came a lull, and while I wondered, the door flew suddenly open and I saw Mrs. Ocumpaugh standing on the threshold, pallid and stricken, looking back at the picture made by the other two as Mrs. Carew, fallen on her knees by the bedside, held to her breast the panting child.

"I can not go against nature," said she. "Keep Gwendolen, and may God have pity upon me and Philo."

I stepped forward. Meeting my eye, she faltered this last word:

"Your advice was good. To-morrow when I meet my husband I will tell him who found the child and why that child is not at my side to greet him."

That night I had a vision. I saw a door—shut, ominous. Before that door stood a woman, tall, pale, beautiful. She was there to enter, but to what no mortal living could say. She saw nothing but loss and the hollowness of a living death behind that closed door.

But who knows? Angels spring up unknown on the darkest road, and perhaps—

Here the vision broke; the day and its possibilities lay before me.